ALL ABOUT SAM

The Life Story of Sampson Buchanan Moxley IV

By Lucina Ball Moxley

GUILDCRAFT OF INDIANA
6000 Sunset Lane
Indianapolis, Indiana
46208

WILLIAM MO

William *b.* 1640 Eng. *d.* Westmoreland Co. Va.
m. 1668 (name unknown)
m. Mary Redman (2nd wife)

William 1670-1744
m. Ann Quigley 1680-1739

Thomas 1672-1702
m. Ann Omohundro

Ann "Nancy" 1674-1700
m. William Omohundro

Richard

William *c.* 1700 *d.* Fairfax Co. Va. 1752
m. Jane Watkins

Thomas *c.* 1700 *d.* Fairfax Co. Va. 1749
m. Ann Gunnell (or Smith)

Samuel 1703-1768 Fairfax Co. Va

Joseph
m. Anne

Thomas *d.* 1806
m. Elizabeth Daniel

Jemima
m. William Whidsor
m. John Piles

Mary Ann
m. Thomas W. Wells

James

John

Sibyl *d.* 1815
m. 3 times
Hugh Ogden
Lewis Cook

Thomas *d.* 1802 Fayette Co. Ky.
m. Penelope Neale

Elizabeth

Spencer *d.* 1848 Montgomery Co. Ky.
m. Milly Thompson *d.* 1852

Job *d.* 1829 Shelby Co. Ky.
m. Mary Buchanan *d.* 1815 F
m. Mrs. Louisa Bell

Nancy *b.* circa 1782
m. Asa Tucker

William *b.* 1797-1872 Oldham Co. Ky
m. Elizabeth Moxley, daughter of Thomas

Mary Ann
m. James Blakemore

Sampson Buchanan 1785-1855 Shelby Co. Ky.

Sampson Buchanan II 1833-1912
m. Marth Venable Payne 1834-1864
m. Sarah Lewis Offutt 1843-1928
(children of Martha)

Mary Ann 1820-1890
m. Wesley Allen Shipma

Paulina 1850-1947

Edward Payne 18

(children of Sarah)

Mary Scott 1869-1946
m. George Armstrong

Sampson Buchanan III 1879-1949
m. Leona Lyons 1888-1984 (div.)
m. Dr. R. Hayes Davis *d.* 1960

Martha 1873-1834

Henry Offutt 1872-

Sampson Buchanan IV 1912-1988
m. Lucina Ball Eckerson

Paulina (Polly) 1915
m. Marshall Bassick (div.)
m. Don Greer

Marshall

Pauline (Candy)

Barret

d. 1668 Westmoreland Co. Va. *m.* Ann Bush

Ann *b.* 1643 Eng. *d.* Westmoreland Co. Va.
m. Richard Omohundro

Richard

776 Daniel 1705-1744 Elinor Margaret Nancy

iam *d.* Boone Co. Ky. 1884
Penelope Neale,
low of brother

James

John
m. Elizabeth Buchanan

Mary
m. Henry James

Penelope
m. James Tucker

Milly
m. John Vallandingham

791-1837 Shelby Co. Ky.
1796-1853

Landel 1795-1865 Shelby Co. Ky.

392
vider

Nancy 1824-1905

George D. 1827-1844

Martha 1883-1906
m. Joel Guthrie

Joseph

Franklin 1835-1837

Hunter 1863
y James Luce

974
s

George Barret 1876-1955
m. Martha Kiefer
m. Charlotte Scott 1882-1935

David
m. Constance Norris
m. Alix Thompson

Gail Cameron Martha Stewart

Barret Scott
m. Doris Blasius

Barret Charlotte Sarah Christina

Irving
m. William Diven
m. Frank Springer

Michael Diven

Library of Congress No. 91-058050

ISBN 1878208-09-8

Cover photos include: Sam sailing Don Greer's boat in the Caribbean out of St. Thomas, V.I.

Sam in Naval uniform at the time of his induction before World War II, 1939.

Sam at his office desk, Haag Drug Co., Indianapolis, Indiana.

Sam's promotional idea for the Indianapolis Symphony Orchestra when he was a member of the Board, took fire. He was made General Chairman of the event. His idea was to bring Jack Benny as guest artist for a benefit concert to raise money, establishing an Endowment Fund for the orchestra's thirtieth anniversary. The concert, under the baton of Izler Solomon, took place at the Circle Theater on November first, 1960, preceded by a gala dinner and followed by an evening of dancing.

Picture of Sam meeting Jack Benny at the airport by *Indianapolis Star*.

FAMILY TREE

The Moxley family, of Welsh descent, moved to England in the 1300s, and three hundred years later some of them migrated to America. William Moxley, born in 1610, his wife Ann Bush and children, William, Jr., born in 1640, and Ann, born in 1643, sailed to America when the children were still quite small. They settled in Virginia near Mobjack, Gloucester County. In 1669, William, Jr. moved to Westmoreland County, where he purchased a plantation of 350 acres. He acquired 192½ additional acres in 1683, "for the consideration of 3300 pounds of good tobacco in casks." In 1744 his son, William III, leased 100 acres in Fairfax County and, together with his brothers, Thomas and Samuel, continued the Moxley enterprise of raising tobacco.

The descendants of those three brothers in Fairfax County, Virginia, are the ones pertinent to Sam's lineage. The direct line issues from Thomas II, born about 1700. One of Thomas's eight children, Thomas III, married Elizabeth Daniel. Four of their sons moved to Kentucky sometime between 1815 and 1820. They were no doubt looking for land to expand their family tobacco business.

Thomas settled in Fayette County with his wife, Penelope Neale, but he died young. Five years after Thomas's death in 1820, Penelope married his brother, William and moved to Boone County.

Spencer and his wife, Millie Thompson, chose to live in Montgomery County, where he died in 1848.

The fourth son, Job, widowed by the death of his wife, Mary Buchanan in 1815, moved with his daughter, Nancy and his four sons to Shelby County where he later married Mrs. Louisa Bell, a widow.

Nancy and three of her brothers married Kentuckians:

Nancy (1782-1834) married Asa Tucker;

Sampson Buchanan (1785-1855) married Martha Harbison, a widow in 1822;

Landel (1795-1865) remained a bachelor;

William B. (1797-1872) married his cousin Elizabeth Moxley (daughter of Thomas III and Elizabeth Daniel);

George Washington (1791-1837) married Catherine Kleiser. They had eight children, one of whom, Sampson Buchanan Moxley II (named for his uncle) became Sam's grandfather.

Of those early Kentuckians, William was considered the roue of the family. "Uncle Billy" was dashing and daring. His escapades were never spelled out, just alluded to in significant tones. His portrait, painted by an itinerant artist, came to Sam IV by inheritance and hangs today in the farmhouse in Shelbyville. It shows a man clothed in a prim black suit, but with an adventurous eye in a handsome face.

From the group of eleven Moxleys in Kentucky the family tree grew many branches, but we are concerned with Job and his children who settled in Shelbyville, now the county seat of Shelby County.

AUTHOR'S NOTES

An interesting development in the Moxley family history came about as I was almost fininshed typing up the final copy of this book. I received a beautifully bound book of 460 pages entitled *Nehemiah Moxley—His Clagettsville Sons and Their Descendants*, written by Allie May Moxley Buxton. Unknown to me, Sam had ordered the book to be sent to him after publication and had included some extra money requesting information about his great grandfather and his two brothers who had migrated from the east to Kentucky.

A few days later a sixty page document arrived from Julian Sorenson in Falls Church, Virginia. He had attended the Moxley family reunion in Damascus, Maryland, in September, 1990, purchased the newly published book and saw the notice quoted from Sam's letter in the Author's Notes.

Mr. Sorenson's letter to me explained he had been researching another branch of the Moxley family for twelve years and submitted the information he had gathered about the genealogy of Sam's ancestors.

I was tremendously excited to receive the document, so that I could include the history in this book. Sam and other members of his family had tried for many years to uncover the background of the three brothers who moved to Kentucky from, they thought, Ann Arundel County in Maryland. They felt the research was futile since the courthouse had burned down and destroyed the family records. But, according to Mr. Sorenson, there were four brothers and one sister who came to Kentucky from Fairfax County, Virginia—not Maryland.

I am happy to have this material to add to my book about Sam. I have made a "tree" (see frontispage) to which the reader can refer and followed it with a brief explanation of how the Moxleys who were pertinent to Sam came to be where they were when he came on the scene.

L.B.M.

DEDICATION

Sam, my dearest,

I am writing to tell you again how much I have loved you. I know you knew this, even though I was unable to say it or even speak to you at the end. Our lives were full and rich with each other. Forty years of love, contentment and happiness fulfilled the goals we worked for and attained together.

What I want to do now is to write what I have learned about you and recount the stories you told about yourself in the days before I knew you. Pictures and vignettes of your growing-up years will bring to life your personality, wisdom and strength of character. I want to do this for you as well as express what I can of my love—perhaps even ease the grief I feel in losing your physical presence. Not to see or hear you, not to touch you ever again except in my thoughts is wretched pain.

I have accepted your death without bitterness, knowing there could have been worse trials for you. I cannot regret the events leading up to the end as I know you wished them to be that way. I am only regretful that you were not allowed immediate release by the doctors who fought so hard to save you. However, those last two weeks gave me time to prepare myself against the terrible shock of losing you.

This story in your memory is for our family and friends who loved and admired you for your generosity, integrity, droll wit and business acumen. You lived up to your belief that immortality is the influence one has on those one touches throughout one's life. This continuity flows on into future generations, reflecting back in memory as pieces of wisdom, morality and ideals, as well as the negative forces. These also have value in teaching the balance of good and evil, right and wrong, strength and weakness.

The seeds of your goodness have been sown in the minds and consciences of many. They will grow and perpetuate your immortality. You will not be forgotten.

Thank you for giving me those years of love, fun and adventure. The memories stored in my mind will forever feed me with happiness. Your love will sustain me always.

'Cina

ALL ABOUT SAM

Sam was nearly born Halloween night, but managed to escape a "spook" distinction by entering the world on November 1, 1912, All Saints' Day, a much more desirable distinction. Sam was far from being a saint, however, according to his playmates. Growing up involved many fist fights and fits of temper—Sam dealing out black eyes and bloody noses and receiving as many in shares.

His life began in Shelbyville, Kentucky, a sleepy farm village of 3,000 persons, located on a highway nearly centered between Louisville and Frankfort. The village boasted an ice plant and a small broom factory, where five or six people were employed making brooms, along with the usual smattering of businesses on the main street—a bank, a grocery, a general store, Woolworth's Five and Dime, as well as the King's Daughter Hospital, which served the surrounding counties. It still operates today as a nursing home.

Every year in late summer, the Shelby County Fair was held at the fairgrounds on the west edge of town. Sam loved the fair and watched, amid the crowd of onlookers, the competitions where the prize farm produce, animals and crafts were exhibited and judged. Housewives worked overtime, canning jars of fruit and vegetables, baking pies and cakes, sewing quilts and embroidering linen. All the best efforts of the farmers were proudly entered in classes of corn, grain, tobacco, fruits and vegetables. Each struggled to produce the biggest melon or pumpkin ever grown and pitted his entry against his neighbors', anxiously watching the judges during competitions. The fair was the event of the year.

Horseshows provided the highlights. American Saddlebred horses of Kentucky are renowned as the finest in the country; featured in three and five-gaited classes, they were combed and curried until they glistened. It was difficult to judge the most outstanding performance as the horses showed off their gaits—manes and tails flying, heads held proudly high.

Celebrations reached full swing at night with square dancing, harness racing and boys' bicycle races. From his earliest years, Sam loved to watch the exhibitions, especially the popular cakewalk competition, which the blacks always won. But his favorite spot was the Midway, crowded, noisy and ablaze with lights. Sam would line up for a turn on the ferris wheel, carousel and other attractions. He tried his skill at the shooting galleries and later became a crack shot, winning medals in contests.

The principal industry in Shelbyville was the raising and warehousing of tobacco. Leaves were tied into hands—a hand consisting of several leaves of tobacco wrapped together with another leaf. Half-a-hand was hung on each side of a hickory stick about four feet long and three-fourths of an inch thick. A stick could hold many hands of tobacco. These sticks were stacked on pallets, graded, weighed and marked with the farmer's name, then put in rows in warehouses ready for sale. Sam joined the crowd of buyers when tobacco auctions were held. The auctioneer walked through a huge warehouse aisle by aisle, stopping at each stack of tobacco to deliver his spiel in a rapid sing-song to the various bidders from firms around the country. Small signals, unrecognized by anyone but the auctioneer, would be given by the bidder. For example, the raising of an eyebrow or scratching of an ear would let the auctioneer know who was bidding. It would end with the final call—"Sold American" or "sold Lorillard." Then the auctioneer would proceed to another stack and continue his spiel until all the warehouses were sold out.

Sam grew up in this community, playing on the farm, scrapping with his playmates and generally exploring and learning about his surroundings. He followed the ice truck on its rounds, (sucking on bits of fallen ice), listened to the tobacco auctioneer, and began smoking raw leaves of tobacco curled into tight rolls by the time he was eight. One would think, from this provincial setting, he would have remained a country boy with small ideas. But Sam had cultured, intelligent parents and from their teachings and disciplines he grew into a remarkable, successful man.

CHAPTER TWO

Sam's grandfather Moxley died without knowing he had a brand new grandson, but he left a widow and many children who played important roles in Sam's life.

Sampson B. Moxley II graduated from Centre College in Danville in 1854. His first wife, Martha Payne, bore three children—Eddie, Katherine and Paulina. Eddie earned his living in the southwest, hauling dynamite into Mexico for mining. He died in the early 1900s. After Martha's death, Sampson married Sarah Offutt and they produced six children—Mary Scott, Henry, Barret, Martha, Sampson B. III and Irving. Sam B. III became the father of Sam IV. All these aunts and uncles except Eddie were influential in Sam's life.

Paulina, called Sister Lina by members of the family, opened Miss Moxley's School in Rome, Italy in 1887. She had taught school in Kansas until she was in her thirties, when she went to Rome. She ran her finishing school for girls until she was eighty-seven, returning to Shelbyville every summer to rest and recruit new students for the subsequent year. She lived through the years of Mussolini's rise to power and at the beginning of his dictatorship was an enthusiastic supporter. Hadn't he drained Rome's swamps and made the trains run on time? But one summer she returned to Shelbyville and reported that she no longer approved of Mussolini. Questioned as to the reason for her change of mind—Did she finally understand that he was a fascist monster and a tyrant for invading Ethiopia? "Not at all," she retorted defiantly, "He passed a law prohibiting men from pinching girls on the street. My girls are beautiful girls, and they are *entitled* to be pinched!"

Sister Lina taught Sam to read before he was five. He recalled how strict she was about pronunciation. When he read aloud the story of "The Little Red Hen," she would insist, "Say *thuh*, not *thee* Little Red Hen. Thee is the word for *you* in the Bible."

Sam's father, always called S.B., was part owner of the Armstrong Insurance Agency, the firm started by his sister Mary Scott's husband, George Armstrong. After George died, S.B. bought a share of the business and ran the agency until he was forced to retire because of Parkinson's disease.

Sam's mother, Leona Lyons of nearby Simpsonville, was a vivacious blonde with a saucy, flirtatious air. She had attracted many beaux before falling under the spell of S.B.'s courtship. Her parents, Thomas Montgomery Lyons and Imogene Webb Lyons, were important to their grandson, Sam. After Leona's marriage, they moved to Meridian, Mississippi, where they bought a lumber plantation with its own mill and private railroad. The train hauled logs to the mill and relayed the processed lumber to the main depot for shipment. Later, Sam's grandparents sold the business and moved first to Pike Road, Alabama, and then to another plantation called Bermuda Hills, near Demopolis, Alabama.

Sam spent many summer vacations in Alabama with his grandparents. He remembered how Grandfather Lyons once gave him the job of driving the mules that turned the hay baler. He sat Sam on the arm of the wheel and showed him how to snap a black snake whip over the rumps of the mules to keep them moving around and around in a circle. For this job Sam received a check for $1.25 for the summer's work. Sam's sister, Polly, found that first paycheck among their father's papers after his death in 1948. It has been saved as a memento.

Once Sam was chased by hornets when he tried to emulate Grandfather Lyons by firing a tobacco stick into the nest. He lit the gasoline-soaked cotton waste on the end of the stick, then found the torch was too short to reach up and push into the nest. The fiery heat maddened the hornets who poured out of the nest and pursued him to the house. "Mama" (Grandmother Lyons), hearing Sam's cries for help, held the screen door open as he screamed his way through it, racing along the hallway stretching to the back door and out again into the backyard without stopping. He collected thirty stings en route.

Leona had an older half-sister who married someone of whom the family disapproved and was never spoken of again. Sam grew up not even knowing her name. Leona's younger sister by two years was Garnette.

Reminiscing about her childhood, Leona told how she and Garnette had their playroom in a large attic room of their home. They divided their play areas in equal shares and jealously guarded their own territory and toys. Leona loved dolls and kept her corner tidy with her doll family's home. She arranged their furniture—a doll bed, chairs, table and a trunk filled with doll clothes which she made with loving care. She presided at the tea table with her dolls; she fussed with the toys, keeping them dusted and in their proper places.

Garnette (Gaga), on the other hand, did not like dolls. She ran a nursery for her pet animals: chickens, hamsters, kittens, puppies and birds. Cages and hutches cluttered her end of the room. The floor was dusted with birdseed and droppings. The pets scrabbled, squealed, mewled and twittered. Leona grew to hate the animals with their smells and constant noise. Once a cat invaded her property and mauled her favorite doll, ruining its clothes. For the rest of her life, Leona hated the very sight of a cat and barely tolerated other animals.

Garnette later married John Walter Collins who owned and managed a plantation and a general store in Gallion, Alabama. Before they bought a home in Gallion, the Collins lived on the second floor of their general store. Sam remembered Uncle John sitting on the front porch of the store, whittling the hours away as he waited for customers. After waiting on a customer, he would return to his rocker on the porch and resume his whittling, reducing a stick to nothing. Once Sam saw him drop his knife and call for a nearby black boy to fetch it for him. Although John Walter was not energetic, he loved to hunt and fish.

A corner of the general store was reserved for a post office, and Gaga became the postmistress of this small community. Gaga and John had a son, John Collins, Jr., who went to West Point and made the U.S. Army his career. He retired as a Brigadier General in 1974. His life would make a separate book of exciting war adventures.

Leona's brother, Wade Lyons, was a man Sam adored. He owned a dairy farm outside of Simpsonville, as well as a general store in town. When Sam was three or four years old, Uncle Wade taught him to add, subtract and divide and to make change for customers. He showed Sam how to use the cash drawer behind the counter and make change from the separate compartments. He looked over the child's shoulder to be sure he didn't give the customer too much change.

CHAPTER THREE

Although Grandfather Moxley died not knowing he had a grandson—the first male born in that generation, Sam's birth was an event of celebration for the family. He was literally the white-haired pet of his many relatives, nicknamed "Snowball" for his shock of pale, near-white hair. But he was small and feisty, with a temper rising to the surface at the slightest provocation from his playmates. Leona became used to her son running home with blackened eyes, dusty, rumpled clothes and bleeding lips. He was often the instigator of the fist fights. Here are some vignettes that Sam recalled:

His earliest recollection was at age two-and-a-half. It was moving day for his parents to the first home of their own. The family had been living with Grandmother Moxley on Magnolia Avenue, sharing the home with Aunt Martha, Aunt Irving and Uncle Barret. It was time for S.B. and Leona to have their own home, particularly now that Leona was pregnant with Sam's future sister.

Toddler Sam remembered watching the movers load their furniture onto the van in front of the house. When the van was nearly ready to depart with all their belongings, Sam thought of a beautiful burnished copper chafing dish, stored in the sideboard in the dining room. It was his favorite piece, but he didn't know it belonged to his Aunt Martha. With much difficulty he extracted it from the sideboard and carried it to the van. Reaching up with all his strength he set it on the tailgate. His toddling away with the chafing dish was soon discovered. His attempt to be helpful was misunderstood, and he was paddled for his interference.

A few months later Polly was born, named Paulina for her aunt. Gaga (Aunt Garnett), visiting from Alabama, took Sam for a walk during the travail of birthing. Sam declared he saw a stork hovering over the house and returning, rushed to his mother's bed. Seeing her asleep, white and exhausted, he panicked and cried over and over, "Mother, please don't die—don't die!"

One Halloween, Sam was left with Daisy, the maid. At dusk he came in from play to see a spook descending the staircase. Daisy in Halloween costume called out, "BOO!" Sam ran out of the house in fright and could not be found for several hours. He often ran away, but invariably returned to Minch's Grocery, where Mr. Minch would perch him on the counter, notify his parents and treat him to something until he was picked up and taken home.

Sam remembered wandering in a deep snowstorm one winter day. He walked down the steps from the front porch. Awestruck by the whiteness and the depth, he made his way to the sidewalk, turned and continued pushing through snow. As he stumbled on, he met the postman, who promptly plucked him out of the drifts, tucked him in his mailbag and continued on his route, delivering Sam at his front door. That ride in the mailbag was an exciting experience.

S.B. constructed a large sand box for Sam between their home and Maud Millerton's. Often, while Sam was playing in the sand, "Aunt" Maud would call to him for a visit. As they talked, Maud offered Sam sticks of chewing gum, which he chewed lustily one at a time. Each juicy wad was relinquished to "Aunt"

Maud's hand, then stuck to pieces of ivy and attached to the wall of the house in order to train the ivy to grow properly.

Red, white and blue? Red, yellow and black? Which colors did Sam prefer? At five, Sam knew nothing about the war. He chose red, yellow and black, the colors of the German Flag. This caused the older boys to cry, "traitor!" and take him prisoner. They locked him in a coal shed for several hours while they went on with their game. Sam was forgotten until his calls for help finally alerted a passer-by.

When Sam and Polly were nine and six years old, Sam decided to teach his sister to play baseball. Unfortunately, he forgot to instruct Polly not to throw the bat after swatting the ball. The bat happened to be a large butcher knife which Sam had found in the kitchen. When Polly struck, the bat flew through the air and imbedded itself in Sam's hand. Leona, the rescuer, began washing the fleshy wound in a basin. Blood flowed and dyed the water a deep red, causing Sam to scream, "I'm bleeding to death!" He kept the scar permanently, but was lucky enough not to lose any fingers.

Uncle Henry Moxley was quite a ladies' man, much sought after as an escort to parties, but he remained a debonair bachelor who devoted most of his time to raising prize Hereford cattle. He was a national authority, called upon to judge cattle across the country. Sam loved to play on his farm. The Scotch herdsman, Mr. Frazer, often perched Sam on "Prince Rupert the 31st's" back to keep him out of trouble while the herdsman was busy at work. Uncle Henry developed the Prince Rupert line of which he was very proud. "Prince Rupert, the 31st" was one of his international champions. Sam once asked Uncle Henry to teach him how to judge. Uncle Henry replied, "I would not teach anyone how to judge either a man or a cow."

Sam admired Uncle Henry's technique of making a sale. Sam was visiting him one day when Mr. Dale arrived from Hawaii to purchase an animal from the herd. Sam recalled Uncle Henry shaking his head sadly, saying he was sorry he had nothing to show him this time but, "Come on in and talk awhile. Join me on the south porch and we'll have a julep. Then I'll show you what I have." After the julep they strolled around to the grazing cattle. Passing one particularly splendid animal, Mr. Dole's eyes lit up and he asked, "What about this one?" Uncle Henry scratched his head and remarked that he had not considered selling him (It was the very one he had in mind to sell).

Back on the porch for another julep, Mr. Dole ventured a bid of $25,000, but Uncle Henry declined sadly. Eventually a sale was made for $48,000—the figure which had already been posted in Uncle Henry's mind.

❦

Sam began school at age seven, the usual age at that time. He was in the first grade for two weeks, then promoted to second grade when the teacher discovered he could already read and do his arithmetic. Second grade lasted another week or so, and finally he was placed in third grade for the balance of his first year in school. His teacher, Miss Sampson, was a hefty woman who punished rebellious students by calling the culprit to the front of the class, placing him on the front row of seats and striking the offender's thighs with an extra wide ruler. Sam attested that this hurt more than a paddle on the fanny. Being a particularly rebellious and obnoxious student, he endured the punishment often enough. The first time he felt the sting, he impulsively called Miss Sampson a name and told her what he thought of her. He was then marched to the bathroom to have his mouth washed out with soap. Sam really feared that teacher!

He was enamored of Harriet Ballard, a classmate with long curls carefully turned with a curling iron. A party was planned for his eighth birthday and Sam was told he could invite as many of his classmates as he chose. When the day came, Harriet Ballard, his sole choice, arrived. They sat in solitary splendor at the dining room table enjoying a birthday party tete-a-tete.

Sam skipped fifth grade and yet another year in high school. In retrospect, he felt it had been a mistake to skip so much. He missed some important things, but in that time and place gifted students were skipped freely. After taking his college board exams, he was accepted at Centre College, where his Grandfather Moxley had graduated.

One day in 1923, when Sam was eleven, he was leaning over to peer into an open basement window of his school. A boy came up behind him and pushed. Sam fell down into the basement and landed on a nail stuck in a board. The nail ran in below his knee-cap, and although the puncture did not hurt much it later caused a high fever. Dr. Buckner, fearing tetanus, gave Sam a therapeutic shot (twenty c.c.s) of horse serum. This caused such a violent reaction that he lay comatose for several days. The doctor advised recuperation in a warm climate, so Sam spent a winter vacation in Florida with his Aunt Martha Golson.

He rode the train to Fort Myers by himself and followed instructions to walk from the station to a wholesale grocery company, there to wait for a Reo truck to take him to Naples along with the bi-weekly delivery of groceries. The truck made its way along the only road to Naples—two tracks of sand with grass straggling up the middle. The only other choice of transportation was a boat. His Aunt Martha had been widowed shortly after her marriage to Eustis Golson and had been one of the first to go to Naples for winter vacations. She built the eighth cottage in that community. Today, her cottage is among those placed each spring on the Historical Tour of "Old Naples."

Sam was supposed to study during the winter, but found he had learned all the material in his textbook the first week. He spent the balance of the season enjoying the beach and Aunt Martha's hospitality. When he returned to school in the fall, he was tested and passed on to the next grade.

While visiting Aunt Martha, Sam discovered some of the devious ways bootleggers outwitted the law. He hung around the pier a good deal and became friends with the fishing guides. He also watched the tourists who had chartered boats and guides for fishing trips. Once he was invited by Red Somonas to make an overnight trip to Bimini. Not wishing to have his aunt "ax" the trip, he sent a black boy with a message to Aunt Martha that he would not be home that night.

At Bimini Sam watched as crates of liquor were brought on board. When the boat was fully loaded, it set off for Naples in broad daylight. Twenty miles south of Naples Bay, Red spotted a Coast Guard cutter a few miles behind and coming up fast. Familiar with all the inlets and coves of the coastal waters, Red ducked into a shallow channel where the cutter could not follow. He then disappeared among the high reeds and swamps. Through the mangrove islands Red maneuvered his boat from Marco to Naples Back Bay and finally unloaded its cargo on the dock. Sam was wide-eyed with excitement over this brush with the law. He asked Red what would have happened if the sheriff had shown up on the dock. Red replied not to worry. He had arranged for the sheriff to be in Fort Myers that day on business.

Red's influence with the law eventually ran out. He was finally caught rum-running and sent to the federal prison in Atlanta.

When Sam related his adventure to Aunt Martha, she only said, "Aha! He has a fresh supply, I'll get some." Things seemed fairly open in Naples as far as the law was concerned. One day Sam wandered down to the beach cottage where another aunt, Mary Scott Armstrong, lived. She had called for a carpenter to fix a dragging screen door on the front porch of her Coquina Cottage, but the busy carpenter explained he would have to send someone else to fix it. By the time Sam arrived, a policeman was working on the door. Soon after, the local bootlegger showed up with several cases of liquor for Mary Scott. There was a false floor covered by a rug in a closet where the supply of whiskey was kept. The policeman dropped his tools and helped the bootlegger carry in the cases. Back to work on the screen door, he spotted a Model T Ford driving on the beach. The policeman rose up, threw down his hammer and ran out to arrest the offender, then came back sputtering:

"Dammit, they don't have no respect for the law! Don't they know it's illegal to drive on the beach?"

The growth of population in Naples was of great concern to Aunt Martha. She told Sam that when she first came to Naples the entire community was composed of about fifty people. She knew everyone and the group had so much fun together. They often enjoyed progressive dinner parties, moving from cottage to cottage, enjoying a course at each place. By 1923, Naples had grown to five hundred winter residents, and she bemoaned the fact that many were strangers to her. "Naples is *ruined*," she complained.

Among Sam's memorabilia is a small notebook. The cover has a pasted-on title in fancy lettering. "SAM MOXLEY'S DIARY—1923 to—." Inside is another fancy-lettered page with the same title but with the addition, "Beginning with his trip to Naples-on-the-Gulf, Florida, 1923, Age 11 years,"

The first page completed his diary for all time:

> *Left Shelbyville for Naples, 15 Dec. 1923. Arrived in Naples, Dec. 19. Met Mr. Pachmeister Dec. 23. Met Cookie Nulser Dec. 21. Grandmother arrived Jan. 31 '24. I went to the beach to see the Gulf. The first water I ever saw I could not see across. There was an unbro-*

ken beach for 11 miles. They were building the pier out to make it 1000 feet. Caddied and made $4.00 later. Judge Wilkerson gave me two turtles. Played with Cookie in his Red Bug. Gathered a collection of shells. Went with Cookie to Little Marco. The first time I ever had been on the Gulf in a boat. Uncle Harry came Feb. 25, 1924. Went out with him in Mack Johnson's boat and the engine broke down. We had to be towed in.

This scrap of written diary in schoolboy script seems to point out Sam's impatience with keeping track of things. He hated to write letters or even send cards at Christmas time. In fact, he didn't correspond with friends except on business, nor write personal memos to himself. All was kept in his head, including social and business appointments. He disdained keeping a budget. He knew where his money went. His intentions were good, but he was soon bored with details, reaching out to grasp bigger, more important things.

Sam's second job (some years after driving the mules) was during high school when he worked at Lynch's Drug Store after school for two hours every day, sometimes delivering orders to customers on his bicycle. He was paid fifty cents a week to supplement his regular allowance of ten cents from his parents. He polished the showcases and windows and became so speedy and proficient with the crumpled newspapers and ammonia that he was entrusted with the dusting of the merchandise, Uncle Barret Moxley had advised him to read all the labels and learn what the products were and what they claimed. When Sam was promoted and allowed to wait on customers, he suffered deep embarrassment when his very first customer, the local prostitute, asked him for a package of Merry Widows (a prominent brand of condoms).

His earnings were spent on marbles, mostly aggies, more beautiful and expensive than the others at twenty-five cents apiece. The boys made a fat box in the dirt and placed the small peewees and larger glassies in the center. The taw (an aggie or steely) was used to shoot at marbles to begin the toss. This could be done standing up on the first shot, but after that one had to knuckle down to shoot at the marbles within the circle. Those shot out of the boundary line were the players to keep, keepers. If not played for keeps, the marbles were just funsies and were later divided up among their owners. (I remember playing marbles, but not outside in the dirt. We played on the oriental rug in our living room, using one of the elaborate circled patterns for our fat box. I remember how contemptuous we were of girls who could not shoot the marbles straight with a strong thumb. When they fumbled a shot, we called them cunny-thumbers.)

In 1927, Sam joined the Boy Scouts, and for two months that summer went on Hillis Howie's Prairie Trek, composed of eighteen boys and three scoutmasters. They drove west in two Model T Ford station wagons and a Model T Ford truck. All the cars were modified with Ruxtell axles for heavy going in mud or sand. The truck carried two boys, the luggage and camping gear. The other boys, with a scoutmaster driving, rode in the station wagons. They left Indianapolis, Howie's home base, and drove to Limon, Colorado, camping out en route, then north to Estes Park for a couple of nights. Then on to Cheyenne to attend the historic five-day rodeo.

From Salt Lake City they continued south to the north rim of the Grand Canyon and crossed the Colorado River on Lee's Ferry, which was manipulated by pulleys, using the river current to power the boat sideways across. Shortly after crossing, they left the highway and drove cross-country through the Painted Desert, taking five days to examine the weird beauty of the landscape before reaching Gallop, New Mexico. Along the way they collected reptiles. The project for the expedition was to furnish the Indiana State Museum in Indianapolis with specimens of reptiles. All kinds of snakes were captured, but the rule was that no boy could take a rattlesnake or gila monster alone. He had to call for a scoutmaster. The boys were allowed to keep the snake coiled and annoyed with a stick until a scoutmaster arrived to kill it. After controlling the snake with two sticks, he would grasp the back of the neck, force open the jaws and run a clipper down the throat to cut the snake's spine. Dead, the snake was coiled, placed in a bottle with formaldehyde poured in to preserve it.

Once Sam found a nest of snakes and carried five of them to a scoutmaster—a snake between each finger held behind their heads. Because their reptile guide book had no reference for that type of snake, Sam received extra points for his catch.

In Gallop the boys camped at the edge of a Navajo Indian reservation. They had an opportunity to talk with the Indians, who were equally curious about the boys and their reason for camping there. Sam remembered entering one of the shelters and watching an Indian melting silver dollars to make his jewelry. Could this experience have sparked his own interest in crafting silver?

The Prairie Trek was in its second year when Sam joined the expedition. It is still in existence today with a permanent campsite near Gallop and is a popular summer experience for both boys and girls. The youngsters now fly to the location, which is presently owned and personally run by Thomas Montgomery Billings, married to Sarah Moxley, a daughter of Doris and Scott Moxley, Sam's first cousin. The camp has grown to accommodate girls who join the Turquoise Trail. A number of instructors lead the youths in archeological digs, mountain climbing and nature studies.

Science Hill School for Girls was an outstanding institution in Shelbyville. It was established in 1825 and operated for over one hundred years. Sam's mother was a graduate and in 1906 followed the custom of scratching her name on the window pane of her room with her senior class diamond ring. Sam's sister, Polly, also graduated from Science Hill, and with the superior instruction added to her native ability, excelled as a pre-med student at Pembroke College (coordinated with Brown University in Providence, Rhode Island). She graduated cum laude, was elected to both Phi Beta Kappa and Sigma Xi, an honorary scientific society. She had spent a year in Rome at Sister Lina's school before going to college. That year in Italy instilled in Polly a great love of the country and a proficiency in the language, which she maintained throughout her life.

Sam felt the women in Shelbyville, particularly those who attended Science Hill, gave the town a high cultural level. They were far better educated than the men who received their education through the local public schools. The men lacked the cultural studies of the humanities—language, music, art, history and advanced English.

The Poynter sisters, who ran the school so skillfully, eventually became ill and were unable to continue. As no suitable successor could be found, the school was forced to close in 1935. The property was sold and two men leased the auditorium to start a gallery of antique furniture and silver. The Wakefield-Scearce Gallery is today nationally famous for its beautiful presentation of exquisite antiques. It has expanded to three levels of showrooms and now fills the entire former school building.

Clockwise (top left) Thomas Montgomery Lyons (Sam's maternal grandfather); John Walter Collins, III, John Walter Collins, Jr., Garnette Lyons Collins; Imogene Webb Lyons (Sam's maternal grandmother).
House on the Shelbyville farm with a family group.

Bottom (l to r) Sampson Buchanan Moxley, II (Sam's paternal grandfather); Sarah Offutt Moxley (Sam's paternal grandmother); Leona Lyons b. 1888 (Sam's mother) and Garnette Lyons b. 1891 (Sam's aunt)

The Moxley Family, Moxley Farm, Shelbyville, Kentucky c. 1923
(Back row: l to r) Leona Lyons Moxley; E. Josephine Smith; Katherine Armstrong; Elizabeth Armstrong McCouch; Martha Moxley Golson; Mary Scott Moxley Armstrong; Charlotte Scott Moxley; Sarah Offut Moxley. (Seated center) Irving Moxley; Irving Moxley, II; Paulina Moxley, II. (Seated Front Row) Sampson B. Moxley, IV; Henry Offut Moxley; Sampson B. Moxley, III; David Moxley; G. Barret Moxley; Scott Moxley; Eric McCouch.

S.B. holding son, Sam IV, at eight months.

Sampson Buchanan Moxley, III.

Leona Lyons Moxley, later married to R. Hayes Davis.

Infant Sam Moxley, IV.

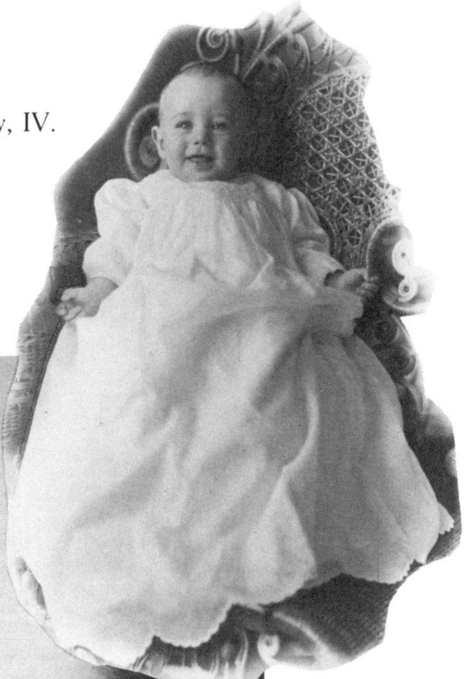

Leona bathing Sam.

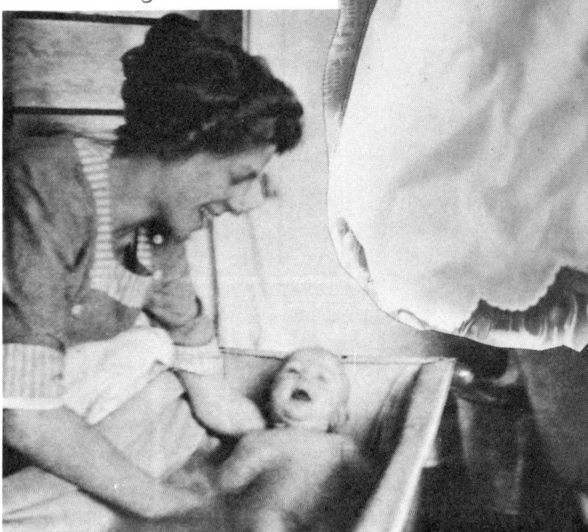

Leona showing Sam off for the camera.

Leona with Sam and Polly.

Sam shown at ages two and four.

Polly and Sam—ages two and five.

Sam at age two.

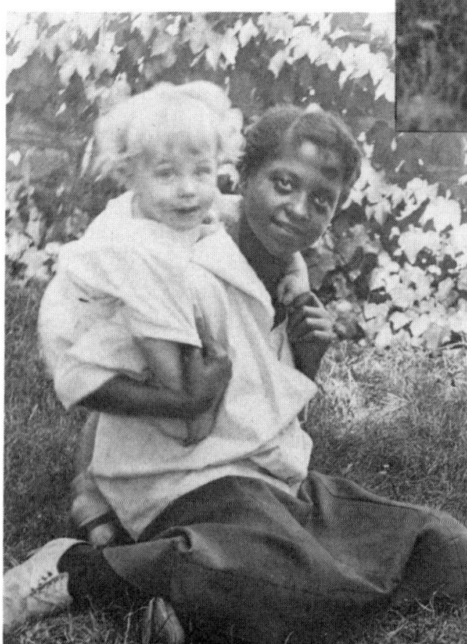

Sam with Thuise.

Polly at age eight.

Sam astride a horse on the farm, age eighteen months.

One of the station wagons on the Prairie Trek, 1927.

Sam was not without musical training. He played a little piano (mostly scales) and some saxophone. Here he is shown with his mandolin orchestra (upper left, top row.)

CHAPTER FOUR

When he was not quite seventeen, barely out of knickers into long trousers, Sam left for Centre College. He had had only eight years of elementary and high school education, weighed one hundred and five pounds, and was five-feet, two inches tall. That year he sprouted nine more inches to reach his adult height of five-feet eleven. He showed a lot of sock below his trousers. Sam was drawn to Centre for several reasons. When he was ten, he had read about the exploits of the famous Bo Macmillan and the great day when Centre's football team beat Harvard six to nothing. Bo was a hero in Kentucky as a football great. Grandmother Moxley, a Presbyterian who wanted Sam to become a minister, encouraged him to matriculate at Centre, because it was a Presbyterian school with a strong ministry department. Besides it was the Alma Mater of Grandfather Moxley.

Immature Sam went to college with his yo-yo in his pocket. He was an expert, but learned quickly he couldn't take his toy to classes. Pledged to Beta Theta Pi fraternity, he was paddled and made to put his attention on his school work. Sam had never studied. He learned everything from listening in the classroom.

Once he had a fight with someone who pushed him from behind. Fits of temper were not tolerated by his fraternity brothers, and when he exploded with rage and struck the shover he earned another paddling. In due time he was initiated and from then on matured considerably with the help of his fraternity brothers.

Important factors in the social life of central Kentucky were the Hop Clubs. These were men's organizations formed in six or eight towns in the Bluegrass region, each club hosting one or more dances a year. Sam was invited to join the Shelbyville Hop Club while still in high school. He had learned to dance under protest while visiting his Uncle Barret and Aunt Charlotte in Indianapolis. Aunt Charlotte insisted that Sam at thirteen learn some social graces. She put a phonograph record on the machine and propelled him around the broad hallway in their home at 101 East 14th Street, Sam protesting all the while that he didn't want to dance with "any old girl." Nevertheless, he learned a rudimentary step or two. In spite of that beginning, he eventually turned into a smooth, enthusiastic dancer.

The Hop Club taught him social protocol and manners, especially how to treat his dates with respect and give them a good time. The Hop Clubs had reciprocal invitation lists. Consequently, attendance involved about one hundred couples and almost as many stags. Parents and older members acted as chaperones and were customarily encouraged to dance by the younger members.

It was the club's pride that each member introduce his date to every man at the dance. They were particularly vigilant to see that any girl from out of town have a whirl of a good time. The stags watched to see that no girl danced too long with one partner. Cut-ins were constant. Supper parties preceding the dances were hosted by the girls' parents in their homes. At this time, dance tallies were given out and filled in. A boy could not monopolize his date by filling in too many dances.

While he was at Centre College, Sam was enamored of a pretty, diminutive brunette who attended Kentucky College for Women in Danville. Her name was Sally McDaniels. She was a tiny girl, just four-foot-eight, weighing seventy-six pounds. Sam couldn't get over her tiny feet and marveled that she wore a size two quadruple A shoe. She was a good size for Sam's five-foot-two (before he grew to 5′11″.) Not many girls were smaller than he at that age. Even Polly, three years younger, had grown to a strapping five-foot-seven. Sam invited Sally to a hop—his first date at one of the dances. She arrived for the weekend at the Moxleys' to share Polly's bedroom. They were dressed for the dance and waiting to leave, but Polly did not emerge from her room. Leona finally went to see what was keeping her daughter. She found Polly in abject despair. "What's Sam trying to do to me," she moaned, "make me look like a *horse*?" It took Leona's best efforts to persuade Polly to cheer up and join the party.

Later at the dance Sam introduced Sally, saw that her program was filled, and as she was dancing took off to dance with someone else. Immediately he was cut in on by two stags, one of whom took him back to the stagline where he received a stern lecture from the older members. There were some men who had not yet met Sally. Before he danced with anybody else he was to see that she knew every man there. Sam groaned. She must meet over one hundred men!

After a year at Centre, Sam knew he was not interested in the ministry and decided to transfer to Purdue University for a degree in chemical engineering. He soon discovered that the subjects were more difficult than any he had previously encountered. His grades began to flounder. He gave up studying and spent a good deal of time playing pool off campus. He became so good at the game he was playing for the house against all comers.

One day Uncle Barret drove to Purdue and took Sam to lunch. He remarked about the failing grades and calmly withdrew fifty dollars from his wallet. Handing the money to Sam he said: 'Take some time off from school. Go to Chicago and see what kind of work you can find there. Then go to Detroit or anywhere else you think you might find work after you are dropped from Purdue. Because if you think you are going home to live off your father, you are mistaken."

Sam was jolted into a sudden realization of the necessity to work. He began to study with intensity, and it wasn't long before his grades picked up.

Uncle Barret Moxley was Sam's mentor throughout his life. He looked up to him with great admiration for his keen business sense, wit and perception. Barret, a true southern gentleman had moved to Indianapolis in 1895. His brother-in-law, Harry Luce, owned the Creamo Cigar Company, and was able to obtain a job for Barret as a cigar salesman with Kiefer Drug Company. Barret's impeccable manners and genial personality endeared him to Indianapolis society. His business acumen came to the attention of Augustus Kiefer. Barret was promoted to a more responsible position and eventually became the company's president. He wooed and won Mr. Kiefer's daughter, Dora, but soon after their marriage she was discovered to be suffering from tuberculosis. Barret resigned his position at the company in order to care for Dora. They moved to Colorado in the hope that the climate might benefit her condition, but Dora died within a year of their marriage. Barret then returned to Indianapolis and the Kiefer Drug Company, at the request of Mr. Kiefer.

Barret's second wife was Charlotte Scott. Their four children were Martha Stewart, Irving (named for her aunt), Scott and David. Charlotte was the granddaughter of Daniel Stewart and daughter of William Scott, who were respectively owner and president of Stewart Drug Company. After marrying Charlotte, Barret arranged a merger of the rival drug companies and the Kiefer-Stewart Wholesale Drug Company was formed. Barret became part owner and president.

CHAPTER FIVE

After being brought up short by his Uncle Barret, Sam successfully completed his sophomore year. During his junior year, however, he began having a series of colds and earaches. This caused him considerable anxiety as deafness was a commom ailment in his family. At the semester break, he consulted his doctor in Louisville and was told that he was seriously run-down. The doctor's advice was that he should drop out of school for a semester and exercise in the fresh air every day by playing eighteen holes of golf and five sets of tennis. Sam complied but grew to hate golf, particularly as his mother could always beat him.

The relaxed interlude gave him time to think seriously about his future. He knew he wanted to work for Barret later on, and he decided to change from chemical engineering to pharmacy. Purdue would not permit a transfer of courses, because he hadn't taken the prerequisites for a pharmacy major. He therefore left Purdue to enter the Indianapolis College of Pharmacy, owned and run by Dean Edward H. Niles. Sam respected this man for many reasons, one of which was his photographic memory. One day Sam was working in the laboratory and got a precipitate from a chemical solution which he was unable to identify in his text book. He left the lab to look for his chemistry professor, but instead met Dean Niles in the hall. The Dean told Sam, "Look in Arny on page 587 near the bottom of the page." Sam looked and found his answer.

Dean Niles had turned prematurely white-haired in his twenties. He was not tall, wore rimless glasses and had baby-pink skin. His philosophy of teaching was that anyone flunking out was a reflection on the teacher, more than the student. He thought the course of pharmacy was not too difficult to pass under proper instruction. He was concerned about one student who was weak in math. He asked Sam to tutor him to get him through his difficulty. Sam did it, of course.

A contrast to this philosophy of teaching came when Dean Niles retired after World War II and Butler University merged the College of Pharmacy into their curriculum. The new Dean followed the premise that twenty percent of the freshman class must be failed in order to uphold academic standards.

Sam rented an attractively cheap room in an otherwise empty house. The room was threadbare and lacked furnishings except for the basic essentials. He soon learned there was a house of prostitution next door on the left and another one across the street. When his mother arrived from Louisville to visit, she was horrified by the run-down neighborhood and the proximity of low-down neighbors. Sam's landlady, who lived next door on the right, assured Leona she liked Sam as a tenant. "He is a nice boy and always takes his girls home before dawn." That clinched it. Sam was told to find better quarters. The truth was he was so ashamed of his room he had never invited anyone into it, boy or girl.

He found a room in the historic Benjamin Harrison home, which he shared with another fellow for a rent of $2.75 apiece each week. He lived there until 1937.

After graduation in 1934, he became a pharmacist at Haag Drug Company. He was paid $14.00 a week. He managed to save $3.00 of this salary and lived on the remaining $11.00. His work schedule averaged eighty-one hours a week, alternating between six a.m. to six p.m. and noon to midnight. Every other Sunday was free. The Sunday he worked was from six a.m. to midnight. Every other week he left a few minutes early and ran to the Lyric theater in order to beat the six o'clock deadline when the price rose from fifteen cents to a quarter. Vaudeville entertainment was featured along with the movie.

Sam's social life included dating a number of girls. He rode the streetcar or bus to their homes, where they would play phonograph records, pull up the rugs and dance. Sometimes Sam would join a friend who had a car for double dating. Occasionally he would splurge and take a girl to a movie. Mostly he stuck to his job and continued to save pennies. The Pennsylvania streetcar took him to work for a nickel, but in good weather he walked the fifteen blocks to the drugstore. After two months, his pay check was raised to $16.00. Then he was able to save $4.00 a week.

Sam learned a great deal working at Haag. He took orders from the manager and his assistant, but he was given a variety of jobs and opportunities to develop salesmanship and creative business ideas. He helped out at the soda fountain during busy hours and learned to make excellent sandwiches. He bragged that he could slice a ham so thin you could read a newspaper through it. Wrinkled up and accompanied with plenty of lettuce and mayonnaise the slice looked like a lot between pieces of buttered toast. He also got the job of window dressing from time to time.

Once Mr. Peckinpaugh, the manager, sent him to a managers' meeting at the head office. He learned quite a bit that day. "Red" Harbison, a vice-president, had just received a batch of night-lights in payment of a bad debt. The lamps were hideous, each made from a conch shell stuck in a glob of green-painted plaster. A Christmas light bulb was wired inside. Mr. Harbison held one of these up and asked how they should be priced. Someone asked, "How much did they cost?"

"The cost has nothing to do with it," replied Harbison, "How much could you get for it?

One manager spoke up, "Eighty-nine cents," Another voice said, "Ninety-nine."

Harbison asked, "What about a dollar nineteen?" They all seemed to agree.

"All right," he continued, "if you can sell them for a dollar nineteen, you can sell them for a dollar forty-nine. How many do you want?" Sam coughed weakly, "I'll take six."

Harbison said, "Okay, I'll send you four dozen. Who else?" There were no takers.

With sinking heart, Sam returned to his store and relayed the information to Mr. Peckinbaugh, who flew off the handle. "*You'll* not go to another meeting. This one is *your* baby. Figure out how *you'll* sell 'em." Instead of the threatened four dozen, six dozen lamps arrived.

Sam took the corner window facing a busy street intersection and built up a massed arrangement using bricks to support four steps with twelve lamps on each step. Connected and lit, all forty-eight made an impresssive effect. The first day, one dozen were sold from an additional display in the store. Mr. Harbison appeared to see how the sale was going. Sam told him it was going so well he would soon have to take some out of the window.

"Oh, don't disturb your display, I'll send you some more." Four more dozen arrived.

The lamps turned out to sell like hot cakes. Finally, Sam retired the last dozen to the basement for storage. A week later, a customer came in to inquire about the lamps.

"I'm from Cincinnati," he explained, "and while here last week I bought one of those shell night-lights for my wife. She showed it to her friends, and they all want one. If you have any left, I would like to have seven." Sam scratched his head, then told the man to wait a minute and he would check. He returned from storage, smiling. "You're in luck! There are just eleven left."

"I'll take them all," said the customer.

The valuable lesson Sam learned from that experience was not to let personal taste stand in the way of selling a product the public might like. This worked well for him in future years when he owned Haag Drug chain and developed a system of feed-back to trigger emergency reorders of fast-selling merchandise.

There were some embarrassing moments with customers. The first feminine tampons had just come on the market. They were called "Wix." A woman appeared at the counter inquiring whether they had any Wix. The clerk replied that, yes, indeed they did.

"What size is your lamp, lady?" he asked.

Standing nearby, Sam overheard the conversation and gently nudged his fellow clerk to one side, "I'll take care of her, George," he said.

A young newsboy, selling papers on the street corner, often came into the store to find warmth on cold, bitter nights. Sam felt compassion for the boy. He was so poor, with thin, ragged clothes. One night he came in with a toothache, asking for some oil of clove for relief. Sam was shocked to see the condition of the boy's mouth when he opened wide to show the offending tooth. Sam called his dentist, Dr. Abrams, whose office was across the street, asking if he would take care of the boy at Sam's expense. An appointment was set. Later the dentist told Sam he had rarely seen teeth in such bad shape from neglect. He extracted the bad tooth, but charged nothing.

Barret had advised Sam to get as varied experience as possible in the drug business. With this in mind, Sam decided to transfer to Walgreen, where he found different management policies. At Haag he had received small commissions on certain items, but at Walgreen he was given a stack of Walgreen items to sell every week. What he was unable to sell he was charged for. Sam pushed the items on the customers diligently, but he did not like the coercion or the sterile, uncreative atmosphere at Walgreen. After six months, he applied for a job with the Hook's Drug Chain. This was early in 1936.

He spent one year at Hook's, working in just one store. In the same amount of time he had worked in three different stores at Haag's. Overall, Sam felt the experience with Haag had been much more valuable than with the other companies.

When Barret offered him a position at Kiefer-Stewart, Sam jumped at the opportunity. He was now earning twenty-five dollars a week, and was able to save eight dollars of it. The more experience he gained, the more he earned. All this time, his uncle had been unobtrusively looking over Sam's shoulder. He had, in fact, been instrumental in getting Sam his first job.

Late in 1937, Aunt Charlotte died. It was then that Uncle Barret asked Sam to live with him and be a companion to his children. The eldest, Irving, was three years younger than Sam and a student at Smith College. Martha Stewart had died in childhood. The boys, considerably younger, were Scott and David.

Sam moved to their home at 1126 North Meridian and worked in the laboratory at Kiefer-Stewart, working up to the position of assistant buyer after two years of experience in the warehouse, which gave him the opportunity to work in every department. Sam enjoyed working there. Though he made the same wage, he had few expenses living with Uncle Barret and was able to invest his hard-earned savings in stocks. He learned much from his uncle. Barret's philosophy served Sam throughout his life.

One day, Sam called on Uncle Barret in his office to get his okay on purchasing a new product. Two of the company salesmen had conferences ahead of him, so Sam stood waiting his turn. When he was finally called into Barret's office, instead of hearing what Sam had to ask, Barret instructed him to look up the history of the two men who had just preceded him. Sam found their records in the file and reported that both men began with the company in 1911 and were paid eight hundred dollars that year. By 1939, they were each earning nine thousand dollars a year. Sheffield, said Uncle Barret, had no children and drove a '38 Buick. He had just come in to ask for a five hundred dollar advance on his commission in order to turn his car in for a new one. All through his career he had overdrawn his account. The other man, Hohmeir, had raised four children, put three of them through college, and had one more still in school. Hohmeir drove a fourteen-year-old Chevrolet. He had come to Barret requesting to invest some additional money in the company. He laid five thousand dollars down on the desk.

"The moral of this comparison," Uncle Barret pointed out, "is that saving is a habit. If each man were earning as much as twenty-five thousand dollars, Sheffield would always be overdrawn, while Hohmeir would still be saving."

Sometimes Barret's small sermons backfired. He took his young sons to a movie one evening, but it was apparent that the subject matter was not fit for young children. He tried in vain to persuade Scott and David to leave the theater before they became too involved with the sex and violence, but the boys remained glued to their seats, eyes riveted on the screen. Barret sat back wondering what he could do to salvage his mistake. As they walked out of the theater, Barret said, "Now you see what happens to wicked men."

David countered, "But, Dad, weren't the wicked women beautiful!"

In 1937 Sam was driving from Indianapolis to Louisville for a debut party at the Louisville Country Club. The car was a Ford sedan belonging to his uncle, with five thousand miles clocked on the meter. Near Scottsburg he was on a long, straight stretch of road with little traffic. He accelerated to ninety miles an hour. At twilight, Sam observed headlights coming toward him. At the same time, a car with no lights began to pass the oncoming car. Sam swerved off the road to avoid a head-on collision, but a parked truck loomed up in his path. He lurched back onto the road, but as he did so the back fender of his car touched the passing car. The impact caused Sam's car to spin into an end-over-end roll. When the Ford finally shuddered to a stop, it was facing in the opposite direction on the opposite side of the road. Sam was able to climb out and assess the damage. The roof was smashed flat to the tops of the seats except behind the wheel where he had sat. His top hat on the back window rack was flat as a pancake and could not be extricated.

Cars were pulling up along the road, the passengers gawking. Sam walked over to the car he had struck, which was undamaged, leaned in the window and asked the driver why he was driving without lights. The elderly wife of the driver looked at Sam and cried out, "He's dying!" and fainted. Unknown to Sam, there was a gash on his head and blood was coursing down his face. Shakily, the driver explained that he was sorry for having no lights. He knew they weren't working, and he was hurrying to pass the other car before it got any darker!

A wrecker arrived in due time and drove Sam into the next town, towing the smashed car behind. Sam phoned his mother, who picked him up at the garage, twenty miles north of Louisville. Hayes, Sam's stepfather, patched up the gash and, nothing daunted, Sam put on his white tie and tails (no top hat) and went on to the debut. It was while he was dancing that he discovered his right arm had locked around the girl. With difficulty, she slithered out from under it, and he gave up and drove home with a dislocated shoulder. At least he had made the party.

S.B. and Leona were divorced in 1934. They had not been compatible for some years and agreed to divorce when Sam and Polly would be in college. Leona moved to Louisville, where she subsequently met Doctor Richard Hayes Davis. They were married in 1935 and built their home in a residential suburb of Louisville called Indian Hills. It was one of the first homes built in that section. Their marriage remained happy and fulfilled until Hayes' death in 1963. He was a tall, heavy-set man with kindness, patience and calm radiating from him. His general practice flourished, and he ran his office and private laboratory with an efficient secretary, laboratory technician and nurses. Many of his patients were referred to him by other doctors because he was an outstanding diagnostician with an ability to spot obscure diseases. He gave of his time to many people who were unable to pay his fee and felt repaid by the healing he accomplished.

One family with several children received constant care from Hayes for a number of years. Hayes knew they were poverty stricken, and he never sent a bill. Then an unusual length of time passed with no calls for his assistance. When he ran into the wife out shopping, he greeted her and said how glad he was that the family was now so healthy.

"Oh, no," she replied. "Jennifer had the flu just last week, and I'm out for the first time in months after a severe illness."

"I'm sorry to hear that," said Hayes. "Why didn't you call me?"

The woman drew herself up and smiled proudly. "My husband has a good job now. We can afford to go to a pay doctor."

From high school days, Sam had discovered a creative release in art. He thought at one time he would like to be an artist. He drew well and had an eye for balance and depth, and a sense of shading and color. He began with a course of charcoal drawing in high school and off and on during his life took classes in various art media. At fourteen, he carved from plaster a nude woman meant to be his mother. The figure, seated with arms folded around her knees, head bent down in meditation was a smooth, perfectly formed statuette. It is kept lovingly among other figurines and miniatures in the glass-fronted cabinet of a secretary in the family home. The amazing thing about the success of the carving is that Sam did everything wrong and in the hardest possible way. He cast a block of plaster in a cigar box, then carved out the figure from the block after it was set and hard, cutting with a pocket knife. The blisters on his hand told him he should have started to carve before the plaster set so hard.

He took mechanical and architectural drawing a few years later at Purdue, and in Indianapolis he took still life and portrait classes from Elmer Taflinger. In the 1950s he resumed Saturday classes with Taflinger, painting life models in oil. He found himself so lost in the work at hand he scarcely knew where he was when time was called to clean brushes and palette.

During his retirement years in the 1980s, he first enjoyed making pottery in a ceramics class at the Indianapolis Art League, and later took classes in jewelry, enamel and cloisonné. In all these media he produced creative designs and well-done pieces—bowls, vases, a set of dishes, pendants and tie-slides.

CHAPTER SIX

In 1938 Sam purchased a one-third interest in a small Rearwin airplane, sharing it with Warman Welliver and Noble Dean. All three were taking flying lessons from Elvin Tarkington and all received their licenses at about the same time. The ninety horsepower plane, a tandem two-seater with enclosed cockpit, cost them eleven hundred dollars. In exchange for hangar use and maintenance work, Elvin was allowed to use the plane for his flying school. The partners received one dollar an hour when the plane was in use for pilot training.

After twenty hours of solo, Sam flew to Brockville, Ontario, where Barret had a summer home on the St. Lawrence River. Sam thought he might as well take a short cut across Lake Erie instead of the around-the-lake route from Buffalo to Watertown, where he intended to refuel. He figured he would climb to twelve thousand feet and reasoned that, in the event of engine trouble, he could glide down and land in the water near a ship which could rescue him. Once over the lake, land disappeared and there was no ship in sight—not even a rowboat. He became bored with the monotony of nothing to see and decided to read a book. Unfastening his seat belt, he turned around on his knees to reach a zipper bag in the back seat. As he unzipped the bag, the engine went "bloop-bloop-bloop." Sam straightened up in a hurry, banged his head on a strut and saw stars. An examination of the instrument panel showed nothing wrong on the gauges. He remembered Tarkington's words of advice: "If anything goes wrong, keep the nose down so as not to lose flying speed."

Sam began to panic as the altitude dropped from twelve thousand to five thousand in a hurry. Just in time, he discovered that the throttle was closed in the back seat. Apparently his sleeve had caught it as he was unzipping the bag. He opened the throttle, the idling engine came to life and the flight resumed.

Arriving at Watertown, he found the field at the edge of the lake, but saw no cars or activity there. He suspected something was wrong and dragged the grass field, still seeing nothing amiss. He was about to land, but changed his mind at the last moment. He climbed once again to a thousand feet and circled the town, looking for another field. On the far side of town he spotted a T-shaped hangar for a single plane beside a narrow grass strip and he landed. The owner told Sam he was lucky not to have landed at the city airport. The whole field was a bog from the unusually high waters of Lake Erie. There was no fuel on the premises, but the man had two five-gallon cans, and he offered to drive Sam to a nearby gas station where they could be filled. After refueling, Sam flew on to Ogdensburg, New York, and landed in a field beside a cemetery. He walked to a house close by and called the Moxley home in Brockville. David was there and drove over to pick him up. There were no unusual incidents on the flight home, but the adventures and near escapes on the first trip were enough to make him wary on future flights.

Still, he had another near miss not too long thereafter. Sam used a small, battery-powered Emerson portable radio to enable him to hone in on city broadcasting stations. He was using this on a flight to Nashville, Tennessee, when the weather changed to rain and low-hanging clouds. The radio advised that the ceiling over the airport was down to eight hundred feet and the field was closing. Nevertheless, Sam thought he had time to make it. On he flew, dropping in altitude as the cloud base continued to lower. Down to just one hundred feet and looking for the airport through the heavy rain, he was startled to see the top of a building go by. He was in downtown Nashville! He pulled the plane straight up in the hope of getting over any cloud covered obstacles that might stand in his path. When he had safely reached five hundred feet, he made a one-hundred-and-eighty degree turn and retreated to Galatin, Tennessee, where he knew there was an emergency landing strip and no buildings!

Leona, fearful of Sam's flying, always cautioned him to "fly low and slow." It became a catchword in the family, but that time it almost did him in. After landing, he waded through soggy, muddy ground to a farmhouse where he waited out the weather with the farm owner attendant. They chatted by a most welcome fire, and for two hours Sam listened to extravagant praise of Franklin Delano Roosevelt. He had become cautious enough not to venture any contradictions for fear of being invited to wait for better weather in his plane.

Sam was born to a Democratic family and was a Democrat until he was almost twenty-one, ready for his first vote. He was still at the College of Pharmacy and often hung around Dorn's Drug Store across the street from his lodging, helping Gene Dorn at the soda fountain late at night so that the owner could check the daily cash intake and record it in his ledger before closing time. It happened frequently that Democrats Judge Kern and Joe Tynan, his secretary, would wind up the day in the store for a cup of coffee and some conversation. One evening, Sam mentioned that he would have to register before the coming election as he would reach his majority on November first. Joe Tynan remarked that it had already been taken care of. He was registered and had voted four times in the previous election. Sam was astounded. At the first opportunity, he checked the records at the courthouse and verified that he actually was on the list of registrants. Sam became an instant Republican.

CHAPTER SEVEN

At the time of Germany's Anschluss with Austria in 1938, Sam applied for a reserve commission as an Ensign in Naval Intelligence. A year later he received his commission as Lieutenant Junior Grade with an accompanying letter explaining that he was too old to be an ensign. He had turned twenty-seven just before the commission was issued.

Sam had sought advice about joining the Navy from Commander Hamilton Bryan, the husband of his cousin, Margaret Luce. Because of Hamilton's advice, he applied for a commission in Naval Intelligence. Later, when Sam asked Ham how to go about getting some training, he was encouraged to apply for a month of training duty without pay in the Panama Canal Zone where Hamilton was stationed with his division of destroyers. Orders came through for Panama on December 1, 1939, but when Sam reported for duty, Commander Hamilton Bryan had been replaced as the division commander. The new officer was surprised to see Sam, but ordered him to report to the destroyer U.S.S. Goff, which was short one officer.

Soon after Sam reported for duty, it became the Goff's turn to provide the senior officer for shore patrol. Sam was sent by the skipper to the Ancon Police Station for that duty. With no instructions or any knowledge of how to perform, Sam was relieved to find a senior yeoman at the station who had been on patrol several times and knew where the teams of men should be assigned. He said the senior officer usually stayed at the Ancon Station with a staff car and four men to be available in the event of trouble during the night.

Late that night a call came through about a major disturbance involving Naval personnel in a bar that was out of bounds for the military. Sam took the squad car to the bar, where he found tables and chairs overturned, some breakage of glassware, but no military personnel. There was, however, a Chief Petty Officer's cap and jacket lying on the floor in a corner. The sleeve of the jacket was solidly covered with gold good conduct hash marks. Sam examined the pockets of the jacket, found the Chief's identification in his wallet and learned he was stationed on a destroyer, which happened to be tied up next to the Goff.

He sent the squad car up and down the street looking for the petty officer and finally found him passed out in a whore's room a few houses away. The unconscious man was loaded into the squad car and driven to his ship. When Sam went up the gangway, he found no duty officer on deck. There was light coming out of the open hatchway. Sam looked in and saw four Chiefs sitting around a table. He told them he needed a working party to get one of their men aboard, telling them his name. The four Chiefs immediately carried their fellow Chief on board, still with no sign of a duty officer on deck.

When Sam returned to the police station, the yeoman asked what he should write in the log concerning the incident. Not having had any previous experience in writing logs, Sam said it wouldn't be necessary to write anything. Because there had been no injury or disturbance when he arrived, he felt the matter was closed.

Later, Sam learned that word had gone around among the fleet Chiefs that the reserve officer had protected one of their own by avoiding the duty officer and suppressing the logging of the incident. From that time on, when Sam was about to do something in error, some Chief would be quick to keep him out of trouble. For example: one time when the Goff was sailing through Las Perlas Islands, Sam was acting as navigator. He took a sighting with an alidade on a couple of landmark islands and drew lines on the chart. The lines indicated they were aground on another island. One of the Chiefs suggested he read the port alidade again. The corrected reading showed them comfortably afloat in the middle of the channel. Normally the navigator would have been left to stew in his own juice.

Shortly after he had reported to the Goff, the District Commandant instructed Sam to go for an interview with the District Intelligence Officer. The officer inquired about Sam's background and then assigned him to report on the Republic of Panama's probable drug requirements in the event of war. Sam thought a good place to start would be with Panama's imports of key drugs, such as quinine, podophyllum and mercury compounds, all of which had been in short supply during World War I. He went to the Panamanian Department of Commerce and Industry and asked if anyone could speak English. He was led to a large private corner office where he found a man who spoke perfect English. Sam asked for figures on the imports of drugs and medical supplies. The man sent for several thick ledgers and let Sam peruse them at a table at one end of his office. Sam had to interrupt the man several times for translations. It took all morning before he finished the last ledger. On his way out he stopped at the front desk to ask who his translator was. He was Señor Arias, Panama's Secretary of Commerce, Industry and Agriculture.

Sam was chagrined and embarrased at having given almost peremptory orders to a person of such importance, so after lunch he returned to the department. Knocking on the office door and entering, he saw the gentleman's face fall in dismay. But when Sam told him he had only returned to apologize for taking up so much of his time, Senor Arias broke into a broad smile. Apparently, Panamanian officials were not accustomed to apologies from U.S. military officers. He ended up inviting Sam to spend a weekend at his mountain resort. Sam accepted and enjoyed an interesting visit during which he met other Panamanian guests as well as Señora Arias.

Another duty Sam had was being the senior officer of a Boarding Party which boarded inbound ships to give them clearance to transit the Canal. He found this was a duty that rotated among the Naval ships in port and that the regular Navy officers disliked it. When the Goff's turn came, Sam got the job. He enjoyed it, so he suggested to his skipper a trade off with the other ships, taking their turns in exchange for some other favor. In this way, Sam got several more days of Boarding duty.

The Boarding Party consisted of the senior officer, a customs man, an intelligence officer, who carried a list of suspect individuals to be checked against the crew and passenger lists, a radio man to disable the ship's radio during canal transit, and some engineers to inspect the ship's hold and, on occasion, probe into fuel tanks to detect any explosives that might be hidden there. The Party went out to sea on a very large launch to board the inbound vessels. If all was clear, the ship was given a special signal to hoist, allowing it to pass the destroyers guarding the entrance to the Canal. Particular attention was paid to Japanese ships, which Sam found to be very clean. He could pass through the holds and the engine room in his white uniform and emerge almost unspotted. The dirtiest ships were the American ones, but the cleanest of all were Swedish.

One of the customs men was named Coffee. Sam told him he would like to learn the technique of baggage search from him as Coffee was very efficient. He invited Sam to go to the customs department on the dock the next afternoon when two passenger ships were due in.

At the baggage inspection the next day, Coffee was showing Sam search technique, when a passenger, overhearing someone address Coffee by name, called out, "Hey, Coffee, get my bags next."

Coffee looked up in anger and said, "I'm Mister Coffee to you." He waved off the other customs inspectors and told them he would take care of the man. He kept him waiting until he was the last passenger there. Coffee then opened one of his bags and began by ripping out the lining. He absolutely tore the bag to pieces. The Chief Inspector came over and suggested he let up. Coffee bristled and asked if he wanted to relieve him of duty. The Chief just shrugged and walked away. This illustrates the power of customs inspectors. Sam suggests never to infuriate a red-headed one named Coffee.

❦

Sam had to answer first call every morning at six a.m. in order to shower, shave and dress in a clean uniform in time for seven o'clock muster on deck for all crew and officers. Afterwards, he would return to his bunk for a little more sleep until the sun rose high enough to overheat his cabin, which was just under the foredeck. The intolerable heat always drove him out of his bunk.

He would then go to the Captain's office and request permission to go ashore. Because Sam had no regular duties assigned, permission was always granted. As Sam would turn to leave, the Captain was apt to say, "Oh, by the way, here is the key to my apartment ashore and a list of telephone numbers for you to call. Get us a couple of dates for tonight. You might go to a market and pick up some ham, eggs, tomatoes and a bottle of wine to have in the apartment by the time I get there around six o'clock."

The skipper and Sam would pick up their dates, go out for dinner and dancing and then back to the apartment for a midnight feast. The skipper was an excellent cook and produced fabulous eggs Benedict. He'd frizzle the ham in Madeira and make a hollandaise sauce to top the ham, sliced tomatoes and poached eggs, which were stacked deliciously on toasted English muffins. After all this they generally returned to the ship about three a.m. The next morning, Sam would be awakened by the six o'clock call and the entire procedure would be repeated. None of the other officers were unattached, and the skipper appreciated Sam's company on parties.

On Christmas Eve, Sam had a date with a girl from Panama and spent the evening putting Christmas lights on a palm tree in front of her house. As far as Sam was concerned, it was a dismal way to spend Christmas. He was homesick. He was happy when his training duty ended a few days later.

CHAPTER EIGHT

Sam's flying days came to an end when he was called into active service in 1941. The partnership agreed to sell the plane. Tarkington made the sale for them, which produced a profit of one thousand dollars. Split three ways, this repaid all their expenses for gas, oil and insurance—plus their flying lessons.

Orders came in March, 1941, for Sam to report to the Great Lakes Naval Station at the District Intelligence Office in Chicago. Sam's assignment was to read the incoming investigation reports and write a one-page summary. In ten days, he had caught up on all the reports and had time on his hands. He began looking in on other departments. One day he discovered Commander Brian Ducey buried under a backlog of work and offered to help him with his correspondence. Sam took a stack of unanswered letters back to his office. When these were dealt with and his own work finished, he returned to Commander Ducey's office with an offer of further assistance if needed. This time, Sam compiled thirty-five paragraphs, a selection of three or four of which would answer any letter. Instead of dictating each answer to his yeoman, he simply marked the pertinent paragraphs. The correspondence was finished twice as fast. After the Commander had received large stacks of letters ready for his signature, he asked Sam's permission to request that he be transferred to his office as administrative assistant. Sam was soon shifted from the Investigative Branch to the Administrative Branch of Intelligence. A couple of months later Commander Ducey was transferred to Cairo and Sam inherited his job. This was May, 1941.

After December seventh, when many senior reserve officers poured in to report for duty, the District Intelligence Officer, Captain Wells, assigned officers who were senior to Sam to other branches, leaving Sam as the officer in charge of Administration. He had thirty officers who were junior to him running the branch. As Lieutenant J.G., he was the lowest ranking officer in charge of any branch of Naval Intelligence in the Ninth Naval District. He kept this job for two-and-a-half years and was eventually promoted to full Lieutenant.

After a few months, the Intelligence office outgrew its quarters and moved from the Great Lakes Naval Station to the twenty-second floor of the Board of Trade Building. Sam was then sharing a house on the campus of the Lake Shore Academy with another officer, Curtis Swift. Later he moved to the Lake Shore Club where he was breakfasting on eggs Benedict on the fateful morning of December seventh when a radio program was interrupted by the news of the Japanese attack on Pearl Harbor. Sam put down his fork and dashed to the office. He was the first officer to arrive and the teletype was chattering. Sam tried desperately to do everything at once until more officers came to help handle the unending stream of calls.

❦

Sometime later Sam moved from the Lake Shore Club to a walk-up, fourth floor apartment which he shared with Bob Smith from Indianapolis. They sub-let the apartment from an actress with the stipulation that her cook was included in the lease. A few months later, the actress wanted to move back. Sam and Bob agreed to give up the apartment provided they could find other quarters and take Frieda, the cook, with them.

Sam set out with a real estate agent to look for another apartment. On the way, the agent asked permission to stop for an interview with a couple who were offering their home for rent. Sam and the realtor walked through the three-story-with-basement house, the agent taking notes as they went along. She asked about the least amount of rent that would be accepted and noted the pertinent features. Sam was impressed with the facility and surprised both the owner and the agent by making an offer. He wanted to rent the house and share it with four other naval officers. Mrs. Sheppard appeared doubtful that her husband would agree to renting to five bachelors, but under Sam's persuasion, agreed to meet with him again that evening when her husband would be present to discuss the matter.

Merrill Sheppard was a top labor lawyer representing several major firms. He told Sam that he had been notified by the draft board that he would soon be called for service. In Sam's opinion Sheppard's experience with unions qualified him for assignment to military government of occupied territories. Sam offered to write a letter to the draft board stating that Sheppard was entering the Navy, which would excuse him from the draft, and then to arrange a commission for him with training in Washington, D.C. This was a much better prospect for the use of Sheppard's talents. He accepted Sam's suggestion with relief and agreed to let the bachelors rent his house.

An interesting sequel to this story is that in 1948, after Sam and I were married and living in Mexico, my parents flew down for a visit, bringing along a couple they had recently met. The couple turned out to be Merrill Sheppard and his new wife, Brenda Forbes, an actress. It was a surprising reunion for Merrill and Sam. They had not seen each other since they were landlord and tenant. My Dad met Sheppard when he was employed by Ball Corporation on a case involving the union. They became instant friends.

The first Mrs. Sheppard was an artist and had done wonderful things to the house at 81 East Elm. In remodeling, the front half had been torn out to make a large two-story living room surrounded by a balcony around the remaining second story bedrooms. A floating stairway half-way back on one side of the room, curving to the center of the balcony, reached the four bedrooms above. On the opposite wall was a large fireplace, the focal point of the room. The dining area was at the rear near the kitchen. It was a dramatic salon, artistically furnished. The third floor had a north-lighted studio adjoining a large bedroom and bath.

Other officers who shared the house were Tom Graham, Ed McDonnell, John Clark, Bob Smith, and Bill "Bug-eye" Graham. Frieda kept house for them. She was given the privilege of hiring an extra maid. The only stipulation Frieda made was that they must let her know by two p.m. if they were going to invite guests for dinner.

The following year provided many happy times for the five congenial young men. Frieda was an invaluable asset, serving excellent meals at their frequent dinner parties. The house ran like clockwork. At any time, with proper notice, the men could invite their dates and fellow officers to dinner, but one time when Sam said guests were coming, Frieda said, "I hope it ain't the same ones you had over the other night."

"No, but why do you ask?" answered Sam.

"Because they ain't no friends of yours."

"What do you mean?"

"The Missus offered me a big raise to come cook for them."

Sam thought quickly and remembered the couple. Elton Frank Motch was a wealthy man. He and his wife were living in an expensive private apartment in the Ambassador East. Mrs. Motch, who was used to every convenience, found herself stuck with the cooking. Sam told Frieda she should accept the offer, as the officers could not afford to pay her nearly that much.

"Never mind," Frieda told him, "I ain't never goin' to work for no woman again. This job suits me fine."

One evening, Sam and a couple of his friends decided to go to a movie in the Loop. When they arrived at the theater, they found a line half-a-block long waiting to buy tickets. Much as he hated standing in line, Sam offered to get the tickets. After twenty minutes of inching toward the booth, he was finally in second place. At that point, a well-dressed man pushed himself into the line between Sam and the customer buying the ticket. Sam was furious at the man's rudeness, but said nothing. He merely dragged a deep puff on his cigarette to redden the butt, then gently pulled open the pocket of the man's tailored jacket and dropped the cigarette in. Busy with the ticket-seller, the man noticed nothing and walked away pleased with himself, unaware of the time bomb in his pocket.

Sam's roommate, Bob Smith, was extremely handsome and attracted many girls. He remained indifferent to them all until Cheer Brentson came on the scene. She was a beautiful, talented actress. As the daughter in a leading radio soap opera, "Ma Perkins," she earned twenty times what the Navy paid Bob. In three weeks Bob was a changed man, head over heels in love. Very shortly, they were engaged.

In the meantime, Sam had become anxious to get out of administrative work and into the "real" action of the war. He requested his District Intelligence Officer to nominate him for an operational assignment. By the time Cheer and Bob were married, he had been transferred to OpIntel (Operational Intelligence) School in New York. After graduation, Sam was sent to Charleston, South Carolina, for a stint in the anti-sub plot room while waiting for his overseas orders.

When Sam reported for duty, his new Executive Officer showed considerable interest in his experience in the Chicago Intelligence Office. The officer said they had just lost the Officer-in-Charge of their Administrative Branch, and he took Sam to be interviewed by the District Intelligence Officer. As a result, Sam was placed in administration instead of in the Anti-Sub-Plot. The job was less important than the one he had left in Chicago. Sam was extremely disappointed.

He found a room in the home of a socialite widow who felt it her patriotic duty to make housing available to military officers. She liked Sam and inveigled invitations for him. He began to be included in many social events. Remembering his interesting experience in Chicago at 81 East Elm, he asked a couple of other Intelligence Officers if they were interested in renting a plantation house with him. He investigated several plantations with a realtor, but when word got around Charleston that a "damn Yankee" was doing this, Sam found he was dropped from the invitation lists. So he killed the plantation idea.

Sam was put on mine-sweeper duty. The ships had very shallow drafts in order to ply the coastal waters with minimum danger of striking underwater rocks or hidden mines. Cape Hatteras is famous as one of the roughest bodies of water in the world, and while on the mine-sweeper Sam became seasick for the only time in his life. He went on deck to breathe fresh air, then rushed to the rail to be sick overboard. The rail was nothing but a cable stretched around the deck. He grabbed it and leaned over. At that moment the ship rolled over forty-five degrees. There he was, under water, clinging with all his strength to the cable until the sweeper rolled back. Half-drowned and totally frightened, he forgot his seasickness.

After three months in Charleston with no sign of overseas orders, Sam telephoned a friend in Washington Intelligence Headquarters, only to discover that the Commandant of the Sixth Naval District had given orders to delete Sam from Operational Intelligence and to assign him permanently as Administrative Officer. The friend said that this request from such an important Admiral meant Sam was stuck in Charleston for the duration of the war.

Sam remembered that there were two regular Navy Commanders in Personnel in Washington who intensely disliked the Naval Bureau of Intelligence and would disapprove of any request for waivers on regulations. He telephoned a chief whom he knew in the mail room at the Bureau of Personnel and asked that he watch for his papers and route them to some other officer for action.

Discouraged but not beaten, Sam requested a three-day leave and flew to Washington to see one of the officers in question. When he knocked on Commander Watson's door, he heard a gruff "Come in." Sam entered and stood at attention while the officer continued to work on papers. Finally, he heard an equally gruff, "What do you want?"

"Sir, I'm stuck in Intelligence and can't get out." Commander Watson's hostility evaporated in a broad grin. He invited Sam to sit down. He asked about his training, naval experience and present assignment. He then told Sam his classification would be changed from Intelligence to Deck Officer and his orders for the Pacific Theater would be in Charleston by Monday. It was Thursday when the orders arrived after much nail biting by Sam. He was instructed to have a physical examination and then proceed to San Francisco for transportation to the headquarters of the Fifth Fleet in the South Pacific.

Sam was feeling ill and running a temperature. He wanted to avoid the physical. He telephoned the District Medical Officer to say that he had had a complete annual examination less than a month before and asked if that report could be put into his record in lieu of a new one. The officer was agreeable and sent a yeoman to pick up Sam's medical record with the new endorsement.

Sam telephoned his mother to tell her he would be spending the three allowed days of "proceed time" with her and Hayes. He left on the night flight. On the plane he began having teeth-chattering chills. The stewardess brought him as many blankets as she could find, and he wrapped up. Nothing stopped the shaking chills. On arrival in Louisville, he taxied home and entered quietly so as not to waken Leona and Hayes. It was two a.m. He hurried to his downstairs bedroom and slept soundly for a few hours.

Upon waking, he found himself too weak even to sit up. He could hear the cook overhead in the kitchen preparing breakfast and pressed a call button beside his bed. She responded right away expecting to get his breakfast order, but Sam asked her if Dr. Davis had left for his office. She replied that he was just going out the door.

"Please catch him before he leaves, and tell him I must see him right away."

The cook ran upstairs and caught Hayes just as he was backing the car out of the garage. When Hayes appeared, Sam told him he hadn't the strength to prop himself up in bed. Hayes began to examine and question him and discovered a small triangle of rash on his chest. He asked Sam to which hospital he could go since there was no military hospital in Louisville. Sam replied that he would be allowed to go to a public health service hospital if no military hospital was near. Hayes called an ambulance, explaining that Sam had either typhus or spinal meningitis. If it was meningitis, speedy treatment was vital. He ordered an intravenous sulpha drip to begin in the ambulance.

The spinal tap in the hospital proved negative for meningitis. Hayes concluded that Sam had typhus. Sam quietly passed out and remained comatose for two weeks.

When he regained consciousness, it was sudden, and he found himself alert, but very weak. Thinking back, he recalled a night he had gone to a movie in Charleston and felt something bite several times on his leg. He had left the theater, returned home and stepped into the bathtub. As he removed his trousers out hopped a flea. He found a row of bites on his leg but was not concerned. He had had his typhus shot six months previously.

For the next two weeks Sam convalesced in the hospital. He had lost forty-five pounds. He tried to eat the hospital food but had no appetite. Everything was tasteless. Alexis, a Russian friend of Hayes and Leona's, came to visit bringing with him jars of his special home-made soup. He requested the hospital kitchen to heat and serve it to Sam. The soup was rich and wonderful and Sam began to thrive from its nourishment. It was the only food he could eat with enjoyment. Alexis brought other flavorful foods from time to time and these meals gave Sam a growing strength.

Sam was required to gain back at least twenty of his lost pounds before he could proceed on his orders to the west coast. As an outpatient recuperating at home, it took him a month to fatten up. Hayes devised a quick method of having Sam drink four ounces of whipping cream frothed up with ginger ale every hour until a quart had been consumed every day.

During that month, Sam became good friends with Alexis. One day he asked him how to concoct his marvelous Russian dishes. Alexis told him to come to his home on a Wednesday morning to learn what he planned to prepare for the Russian Easter festival on the coming Sunday. Sam showed up before ten a.m. and Alexis fixed highballs for them. By noon they were on their third highball, but no cooking preparations had begun. Sam ventured to ask what they were going to make. Alexis told him that piroshkis, pasha and kulich were the important foods at the Easter celebration. He listed the ingredients while they continued to drink.

When Alexis suggested he make them yet another high-ball, Sam asked if they shouldn't start the cooking. Alexis said, "Well, go in the kitchen and start." Sam protested that while Alexis had told him what the ingredients were, he had not said how much of anything to put in. "But," Alexis retorted, "in Russian cooking there are only three quantities: a little, some and a lot. The charm of Russian food is that it never comes out the same."

Without further specifics to help him, Sam went out to the kitchen and began to make the piroshki dough. He lucked out with only one hint from Alexis to roll the dough a little thinner. The piroshkis were good.

Finally, he was able to proceed to San Francisco. That summer of 1943, Sam boarded the U.S.S. Exiria for the South Pacific. The ship followed a circuitous route south of Tonga and arrived more than three weeks later in Numea, east of New Guinea. He was put on a small oil tanker headed for the Solomon Islands and given orders to report to the Commander of the Tulagi Florida Island area.

After arrival at Tulagi, he stashed his gear on the dock and walked around asking questions. He wanted to find out what was going on. He learned that he was in a staging and supply area for ships preparing for invasions of other islands. A new commander had just taken over the day before.

Sam made his way in to report to the Executive Officer, Arnold Nall. While he was reporting, the new area Commander walked in and Sam was introduced. Captain Ross showed a glimmer of recognition: "Moxley—Moxley? Were you in Naval Intelligence in Chicago?" When Sam replied affirmatively, Captain Ross reminded him that he also was there as the Commanding Officer of the Navy Pier Training Activities and had called Sam several times to discuss various problems. He then turned to Commander Nall and said, "Don't assign Moxley any duties. I'll have something for him later."

This was the beginning of Sam's tour of duty in the South Pacific, which he later described as "a bed of roses." He felt the luck of the world was with him and proceeded to enjoy the time spent at his posts. One of Sam's duties was heading the officers' mess. He planned appetizing meals in spite of the limited quality of produce and meats. Plenty of mutton was sent from New Zealand, but the men would not eat it. When a ship arrived with a load of lamb or mutton, the unloading crew calmly heaved it overboard into the sea. When Sam saw the meat floating out with the tide, he thought hard about a method for salvaging some of it. He created a recipe which would disguise the flavor of mutton and served it under an exotic name. An appetizing casserole appeared on the menu, well spiced with herbs and laced with curry. The mutton was diced into tiny bits, cooked until very tender and mixed with the available vegetables and rice. No one was the wiser and seconds were called for.

Another time, he had a great idea for Thanksgiving dinner. Since there were plenty of palm trees on the island, he thought hearts of palm would make a terrific salad. He ordered one of the bulldozers that were working on the air strip to knock down a palm tree. The salad was a success, but news of the tree loss reached British Headquarters. They promptly sent a bill for $700. Sam was reprimanded and that was the last of the gourmet salads.

CHAPTER NINE

The war was over. Sam had been in the service for six years, starting out as a Lieutenant J.G. and ending as a Lieutenant Commander. He was made a full Commander in 1948 while living in Mexico.

Among papers stored as memorabilia from World War II are several reports which reveal much about Sam's character as well as explaining his duties in the Pacific. Sam was awarded the Bronze Star. The letter of commendation came from captain Charles E. Lee, Commander of Fleet Air Wing Eighteen:

> *Lieutenant Commander Moxley was assigned duty under the Command Naval Base, Tulagi from 4 June, '44 to April 7, '45. As Administrative Assistant to the Commanding Officer, he suggested, organized and supervised a Central Transportation Pool for all base activities and materially increased the ability of the base fleet units staging in the area. He also conducted many investigations for the Commanding Officer; the Senior Member of various Boards of Investigation, Courts of Inquiry and Summary Courts Martial. He was Senior Member of Auditing Boards and established procedure for auditing the Fleet Recreation Center, Ship's Service Activities, all Officers' Messes and Wine Messes in the area, and was a member of the Board of Governors and of the Audit Board of the Iron Bottom Bay Club. As Equipment Maintenance Officer, he greatly improved the operating condition of aging equipment in the area and reduced the number of accidents.*
>
> *From 23 May to 1 October '45, he was assigned duties as Awards Officer and Administrative Officer for the Command Fleet Air Wing Eighteen, in addition, on 22 July, '45, being designated as Flag Secretary and Flag Lieutenant, he exhibited fine qualities of initiative and judgment in the execution of his duties. His efforts on the Awards Board lessened materially the difficulties experienced by the squadrons*

in securing proper awards for the personnel, a backlog of approximately thirty-five hundred recommendations being acted upon during this period.

The citation when Sam was awarded the medal said this:

In the name of the President of the United States, the Commander Fleet Air Wing Eighteen takes pleasure in presenting the BRONZE STAR MEDAL *to* LIEUTENANT COMMANDER SAMPSON BUCHANAN MOXLEY UNITED STATES NAVAL RESERVE *for service as set forth in the following* CITATION:

For distinguishing himself by meritorious achievement during the period of 4 June, 44 to 1 October, '45. As Administrative Assistant to the Commanding Officer, Naval Advanced Base Tulagi, he materially contributed to the ability of the base in meeting its logistic support function during four major task force stagings. As Flag Secretary and Awards Officer of Fleet Air Wing Eighteen, he performed essential administrative duties in an outstanding manner. His conduct and initiative were at all times in keeping with the highest traditions of the United States Naval Service.

M.R. Greer, Rear Admiral, U.S. Navy

When Sam requested release from duty at the conclusion of the war, Admiral Greer made out the report, adding a concise appraisal of Sam and his performance of duty.

Lieutenant Moxley is an outstanding officer. He is of excellent moral and military character. He had an excellent knowledge of his job. He has a pleasing personality and is a good mixer. He is efficient and has performed all duties assigned him in an excellent manner. He is highly recommended for promotion in the U.S.N.R. when due. Since he had requested release from active duty he is not recommended for retention. This officer has been shown this fitness report.

Sam's separation papers arrived on September 17, 1945, and on November 7 his certificate of satisfactory service was sent from James Forrestal, Secretary of the Navy, with an accompanying letter:

My dear Mr. Moxley,

I have addressed this letter to reach you after all the formalities of your separation from active service are completed. I have done so because, without formality but as clearly as I know how to say it, I want the Navy's pride in you, which it is my privilege to express, to reach into your civil life and remain with you always.

You have served in the greatest Navy in the world. It crushed two enemy fleets at once, receiving their surrenders only four months apart. It brought our land-based airpower within bombing range of the enemy, and set our ground armies on the beachheads of final victory. It performed the multitude of tasks necessary to support these military operations. No other Navy at any time has done so much. For your part in these achievements you deserve to be proud as long as you live. The Nation which you served at a time of crisis will remember you with gratitude.

The best wishes of the Navy go with you into civilian life. Good Luck!

Sincerely yours, James Forrestal

Another piece of correspondence I found tucked in the thick portfolio of papers relating to his six years of duty in the Navy was a letter to the Chief of Naval Personnel in Tulagi, dated September 11, 1944:

It is respectfully requested that I be ordered to a Fighter Director School and subsequently assigned C.T.C. duty on an aircraft carrier.

It is believed that my experience in owning and flying an aeroplane before entering the Navy, a minimum experience in municipal airport control tower operation, completion of the Operational Intelligence School, experience in maintaining the anti-sub operation plot in the Southern Sector of Eastern Sea Frontage, with three years active duty in Naval Intelligence presents a desirable background for the Fighter Director School.

In addition, it is believed that my service in this requested combat duty would be of greater value to the Navy than my present Advanced Base Duty.

S. B. Moxley

The fact that Sam was denied this duty speaks well of his Commanding Officer, who knew how much he was needed on the base and countermanded the request. The letter was a surprise to me because Sam never told me that he had tried hard to get out of administrative offices and into active combat after he was sent to the South Pacific.

Sam in High School.

Sam in College.

Note the little statuette on the table behind Polly, which Sam carved out of plaster to represent his mother.

Leona in the early 1930's.

The wrecked Ford, 1927.

Commander Sam B. Moxley.

Sam's office personnel.

Commander B. O. Wells; Lieutenant Commander Thomas Cullen; Sam Moxley.

Ensign Robert M. Smith.

Ensign William (Bug-eye) Graham; Ensign Ed McDonnell (killed during W.W. II) Ensign Robert Smith; Lieutenant J.G. Sam Moxley.

Some of Sam's war-time girl friends: (l to r) Dawn Arnall, Wellington, New Zealand 4/20/45;

Sam with unknown date;

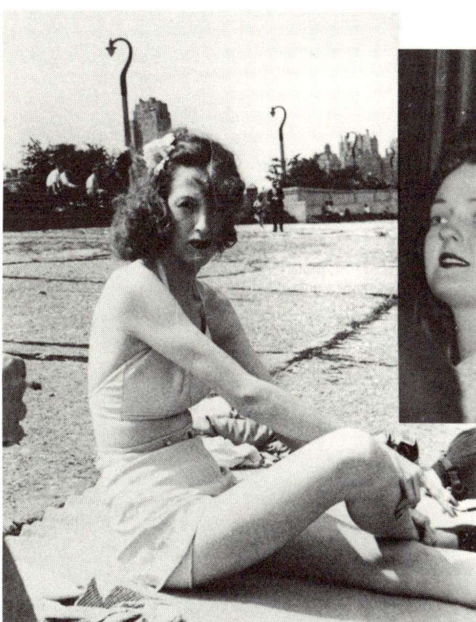

Judy Keyes, Chicago, Illinois (this was a near miss for me as Sam almost married her).

Unknown beach girl;

Destroyer U.S.S. Goff in Panama, where Sam was first stationed in 1939.

(Top) Tent city in Tinian, South Pacific. (Middle) Sam with two friends. Ted Cummerford is at left. (Bottom) Post Exchange, Tinian.

Aircraft Carrier, South Pacific Theater, W.W. II.

Plane on fire coming in to carrier.

Sam with the Skipper, Admiral Greer and unidentified friend.

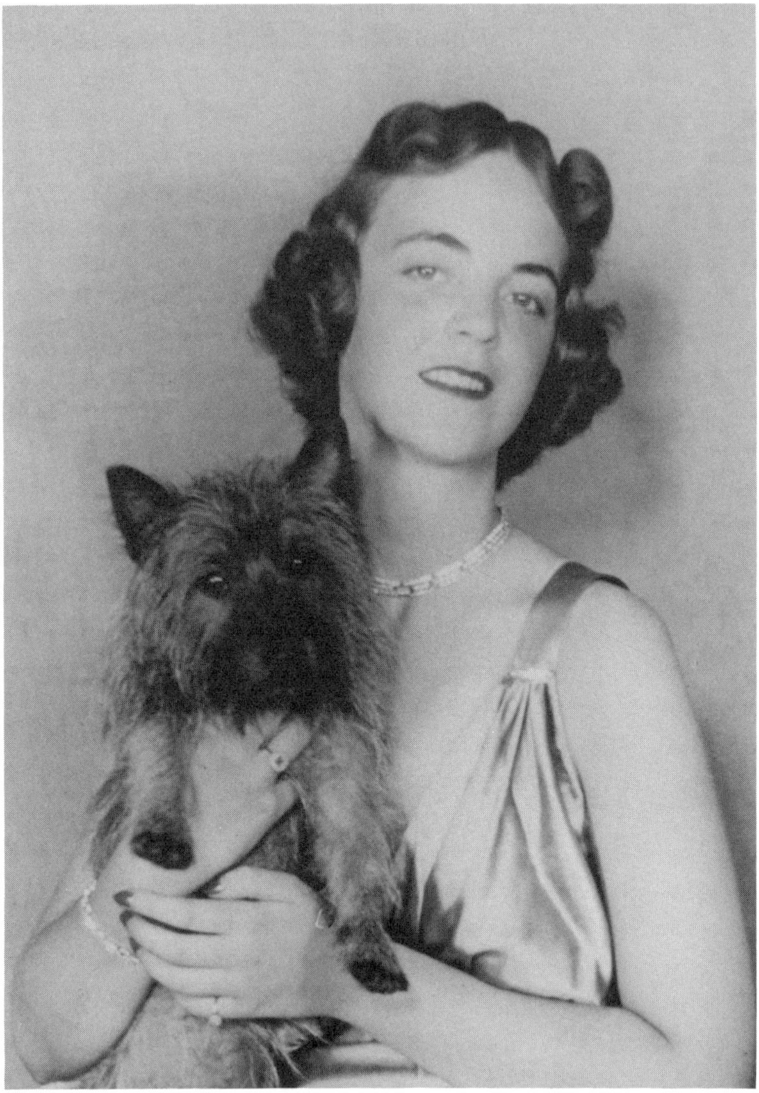
Polly during college years with family dog, Dockie.

Polly with her children, Marshall, Candy and Barret, 1948.

Polly marries Don Greer in Louisville, Ky. Christmas 1969. Leona is between them.

Paulina Moxley (Polly) Bassick, John Walter Collins III, Adrienne (Candy) Bassick c. 1960.

Polly with her grown children in Hyannisport, MA. 1978. Marsh, Candy and Barret.

Polly and Don, 1991.

WESTERN UNION

(30)..

1945 OCT 12 AM 12 15

AA 14

A.FA938 9=SANFRANCISCO CALIF 11 849P

MRS R HAYES DAVIS=

INDIAN HILLS PHONE TAYLOR 4143 LVILLE=

CLIFT HOTEL SAN FRAN NOW HOME ABOUT TWENTIETH LOVE=

SAM.

(Clockwise) David Moxley during World War II; Scott Moxley, age about 13; Sam's telegram to Leona anouncing his return from the Pacific Theater after W.W. II—October 12, 1945. G. Barret Moxley. Irving Moxley with Sam.

R. Hayes Davis, Sam's step-father.

CHAPTER TEN

Before returning to Louisville or Indianapolis, Sam planned a terminal leave in Mexico City with fiestas and siestas. Hayes and Leona had told him enough about the country and their visits with Marguerite and Axel Wenner-Gren to whet his enthusiasm to see for himself what Mexico had to offer. Marguerite was a distant cousin of Hayes and Sam was instructed to pay the Wenner-Grens a courtesy visit. Beyond that, Sam had no intention of spending time with them. His interest lay in chasing girls in the cantinas.

After a delayed plane arrival and a lengthy trip through customs, Sam arrived about midnight to claim his reserved room at the Reforma Hotel. The desk clerk informed him that his room had been cancelled by Senor Wenner-Gren, who was expecting him as a guest at his home. Tired and irritated by this news, Sam insisted that another room be found for him. But the Reforma was full and the clerk's telephoning produced nothing available in other hotels.

Very much out of sorts, Sam finally taxied to 390 Paseo de la Reforma and rang the bell. It was two a.m. A butler, fully dressed and wide awake, opened the door and escorted Sam to a bedroom in the mansion and told him that Senor Wenner-Gren requested his presence at breakfast.

Fortino, the butler, would awaken him at seven. Sam gnashed his teeth. After the long flight from San Francisco, all he wanted was at least eight or ten hours of sleep.

When he met Axel the next morning, however, he found him both fascinating and formidable. Axel was tall, an erect handsome figure with a thick shock of white hair and penetrating ice blue eyes. He also had a magnetic voice accented with a delightful musical lilt, typical of the Swedish sing-song. He charmed Sam immediately, even though Sam realized this man was razor sharp, quick to pick the brains of friends or adversaries. Axel had made his fortune in the manufacture and sales of Electrolux vacuum cleaners and Servel refrigerators. He acquired other businesses with as much ease as pouring peanuts into his palm. When Sam met him, he was listed among the top five richest men in the world.

The Wenner-Grens had escaped from Europe at the beginning of the war, just before the Swedish government froze the sale of oil to civilians. Axel fueled his yacht, the Southern Cross, and slipped out one night with a full crew, intending to move to the United States. The second night at sea they heard an SOS on their radio and headed toward the British liner, Athenia, which had been torpedoed by a German submarine. They found hundreds of passengers from the sinking ship swimming and drowning in the frigid North Sea. They managed to pull about two hundred aboard their ship, while others drowned only inches from safety. All the linen on the ship was torn up to make bandages for the injured, and the crew was busy day and night administering first aid. This was the first passenger ship sunk by the Germans in World War II.

The Southern Cross headed for Halifax and unloaded the survivors, not daring to enter the mine-filled English Channel. The yacht then proceeded towards New York, only to learn from the ship's communication that Axel had been put on a blacklist in the United States because of political rumors about him which were unfounded. Deeply offended and outraged, Axel changed course for Vera Cruz, Mexico.

Axel told Sam that when they had arrived in Vera Cruz and he inquired about shipping his goods to Mexico City by railroad, he was advised to hire Mexican peons to carry the furniture to the capital on their backs. Axel was dumbfounded and argued that it was a six-hundred-mile journey up the mountains to Mexico

City. How could a man possibly carry a bed, a dining table, a desk or any of the heavy oak pieces uphill into an altitude of 7200 feet? He was told the peons did this kind of work regularly, that they were desperately poor and would be glad to have the work. So it was that over one hundred men walked to Mexico City with furniture and trunks strapped on their backs to transport the contents of the Southern Cross to the capital. In return, Axel gave the yacht to the Mexican Navy.

Sam was invited to accompany Axel on his round of business inspections, and together they were driven by Axel's chauffeur to the Banco Continental, Lecheria Nationalc (a milk pasteurization plant), Paracina (a jewelry factory), Decor (an interior decorating shop), Conquistador S.A. (a silver factory), Mexicana and Ericson (telephone companies), and Latino Americana (an apartment hotel).

After the drive, they returned to the residence in time to dress for dinner. Formal attire was mandatory in the Wenner-Gren household. Sam wore his white dress uniform, which made a big impression on Marguerite. When goodnights had been said, Sam set out to explore Mexican night life.

Wakeup call came again at seven a.m. after a two hour nap, and the previous day's routine was repeated. This ritual went on every day and night of Sam's terminal leave. Youth and determination allowed him to manage quite well on two hours of sleep a night.

Meanwhile, Axel had offered Sam a position with one of his companies, Lecheria Nationale. He seemed to recognize in Sam a talent for business organization and to see him as a trouble shooter, one who could bring a company out of debt and into profit-making. Axel's idea was to place Sam on the boards of several troubled companies and to have him work actively with one of them until it could operate successfully. When this was accomplished; Sam would be moved to another faltering enterprise. Axel promised him an exciting international life with unlimited opportunities for reaching the heady goal of millionaire in a few short years. Sam had to think this over. He returned to Indianapolis, promising Axel an early reply.

CHAPTER ELEVEN

When I met Sam, he was deep in thought over this proposal, knowing it would be a decision that would alter his life as well as his career. Now was the time to begin something new if he ever would. He knew he would not advance at Kiefer-Stewart because Barret's sons, David and Scott, would eventually take precedence and would come to own the business. It was better not to resume his former job with Kiefer-Stewart after the six year lapse, unless he could commit himself to it. Axel's offer presented an opportunity to attain a position of authority. Now was the time to make the break, but it was hard to choose between the security of the family business in familiar surroundings and a risky adventure in a foreign country whose language and culture he was unfamiliar with. The challenge was there and he dared to accept it.

This was what first attracted me to Sam. I admired him greatly for his ability to pull up stakes in a "safe" future and head for an adventure of unknown dimensions. Although I had known Sam slightly through my parents' friendship with Barret Moxley, we had never dated until I became a widow. My husband, Ed Eckerson, had been Chief of Surgery on the hospital ship, Comfort, when it was kamikazied off Okinawa in April, 1945. His death left me with two little girls, ages two and four, living in Muncie near my parents. Possibly prodded by his uncle Barret, Sam invited me to attend the Hunt Ball with him in Indianapolis and this is how we became acquainted. The three times we were together he voiced his thoughts, the pros and cons, the questions that had no answers, and his wavering doubts. He needed someone to listen, and talking helped him to find the answers.

I left Indiana winter behind me on January 2, 1946, and flew to Arizona, taking my daughters, Judy and Ann, with me. Mother and Dad traveled with us, flying in Dad's twin Beechcraft plane. In those days when Dad owned a plane, it was fun and easy to plan trips. Dad loved to go anywhere, and the least excuse would give him wings, lifting Mother and anyone else who wished to grab his coattails to fly along. Dick Whitney was his pilot. He flew us north, south, east and west for many years.

I planned to be at Jokake Inn north of Phoenix in the area now called Scottsdale for three months. I did not know what decision Sam finally made until he called me from San Antonio late in January to say he was on his way to Mexico. He left his Buick convertible, with a trailer filled with his possessions hooked on to it, to be checked over before the grueling drive to Mexico City. He then flew to Phoenix to see me once more before crossing the border.

I was pleased that he flew such a long distance to be with me for such a short time. We only had two days to be together, but the time was pleasant, comfortable and relaxed. I was surprised that Sam was not more excited to be off on such an adventure, but I learned later that he was not one to show emotion. He held the turmoil of thoughts and plans within himself. He had made his decision and now, like Dorothy, was off to see the wizard.

It was a year-and-a-half before I saw Sam again. During that span of time only two or three letters passed between us. I moved back to New York in April, 1946, where I had lived before the war with my doctor husband, and wrote Sam a note to give him my new address. He responded much later, but warmly, with the news of his experiences. He was assistant manager of Lecheria Nationale. This company had powdered milk shipped in from Wisconsin, added sterile water and the proper amount of bacteria to insure against spoilage, and then distributed the milk throughout the city. It was the only milk in Mexico which was safe to drink without first being boiled.

In February, 1948, I sent Sam a Valentine with a plea to be my Valentine "in absentia." The response came back immediately, "I do not wish to be your Valentine in absentia. I'm coming to New York on February 27 to see you in person." The letter and Sam arrived the same day. Two days later we were engaged. It was a surprise to both of us, as well as to our families. Sam laughed and joked that he had always been able to propose to a girl on the third date, knowing that she would refuse, but that he would get "Brownie points." Here I was on the third date saying "yes" without hesitation.

Somehow, I knew our life together would be compatible at the very least. Sam wanted to chance it, but I felt he had reservations about being married. He was fond of saying he had always been able to ride a bicycle backwards. (Could get to the point of proposing then back off in a hurry). At thirty-six, he was still a happy bachelor, and it was hard for him to tie himself to just one girl for a lifetime. The experience I had had of five years of married life gave me confidence that I could make Sam happy. I admired and respected him, and I tingled all over with excitement and anticipation just being with him.

Sam told me he was attracted to me by the way I handled my widowhood. He admired me for meeting my grief head-on, facing problems practically. With two little girls to raise, it seemed to me there was no choice but to do the best I could to give them all the love and attention possible. I was lonely, angry and bitter over the war's ruthlessness, but what could I do except live each day and plan for their future? I was resigned to my loneliness and did not expect to fall in love again. It was a shock to discover I had fallen in love with Sam.

After we were married, I learned about Sam's family background with vignettes of his growing-up years. His family was as extensive as mine, but we weren't burdened by the overdose of relatives. In fact, we amused each other with tales about our ancestors, their eccentricities and accomplishments. Sam was proud of his heritage as I was of mine. We both had learned valuable lessons in deportment and morals from our Victorian models. I am glad to say we benefited by emulating the lifestyles of those we admired. So, with similar beliefs and modes of conduct, we were well suited to each other, even though we were quite diverse in our personal interests. Sam was absorbed in economics, investments, and any problems related to mathematics or science. I followed the arts and humanities, particularly music, which is my driving force. I love teaching and studying music, art and history. We balanced nicely, followed our own interests and learned about each other's.

The details of our courtship and marriage are written in my autobiography, *Recollections of Lucina—The Best Years*. I finished the book in 1984. Therefore, I will sketch the important events leading up to that time, then complete our life together which lasted just four more years. Reflecting back over forty years of marriage, I realize how much Sam loved me. When he was financially able, nothing could stop him from giving me gifts of lovely jewelry, treasures of souvenirs from our many trips and improvements to our home to make it more and more comfortable. He was not only willing, but anxious to give me anything I wanted, and it upset him when I didn't want anything. I was happy with all I had, content and fulfilled just to be with Sam. He was the one with the driving urge to travel and would have done more of it if I had not held him back.

When our family toured Europe in 1953, it was the first time for Sam, but it whetted his desire to see everything "before I am on crutches," meaning before he was too old. His first taste of adventure was in the South Pacific during World War II. Living in Mexico was the next. He learned a new language, familiarized himself with a new culture, and became addicted to the exotic, ambient life of leisure combined with hard work that was so beautifully adopted by the Mexicans. Still, trips were few and far between until he retired in 1972, when he tried to make up for the many years he had denied himself that pleasure because of his career. Everything he had he made on his own, beginning with his first salaried job in 1932 when he struggled to save $4.00 out of his paycheck.

Before we were married Sam had seriously considered other commitments. The last attraction he had was for a fascinating Mexican girl. Chata Serano was a vivacious blonde, one of eight children from a prominent Mexican family. Chata (a nickname for pug nose) was allowed to date Sam, provided a chaperone accompanied them. As the courtship progressed, Sam's ardor and frustration increased, and he decided to propose. But how was he to get the girl alone? The Mexican social custom of chaperones was quite strict, and Sam didn't know how to get around it.

One evening, parted from the chaperone while they danced, he asked Chata how they could escape from the beady-eyed surveillance of a third party.

"No trouble at all," she replied, "since I am allowed family members as chaperones my older brother can go with us. Right now he is dating a girl he likes very much and will want to be alone with her. That will give us a chance to be alone too."

Sam began making plans for their next date, but Chata sensed that Sam was getting serious, and turned the conversation to her family:

"Isn't it a shame that families these days are getting smaller and smaller? My great grandparents had fourteen children, my grandparents ten, but my parents *only* had eight."

Sam's ardor cooled rapidly. He thought, "This is no league for Moxley."

❦

In Mexico it was customary to bargain with storekeepers. One was never foolish enough to pay the asking price without first arguing over it. Sam often bought oranges from the poor people sitting on street corners and spent a good deal of time wrangling the price down from five or ten pesos to one or two. One time he walked away with his bag of oranges, bought from a ragged old lady sitting on the pavement.

Suddenly, it struck him that he had spent ten minutes "stealing" her oranges for half price, but that the night before he had gone to an elegant restaurant and paid for his dinner, adding a big tip without a qualm. He was ashamed of himself and never again bargained with a poor or handicapped person trying to eke out a living by selling some merchandise.

CHAPTER TWELVE

On Leap Year night, February 29, 1948, we became engaged, and from that moment on excitement mounted for both of us. Sam delayed his return so that it would coincide with my vacation in Nassau during Judy's spring vacation from Brearley School, where she was enrolled in first grade. It was sheer coincidence that Sam had planned to fly to Nassau also. The Wenner-Grens owned Hog Island (now more picturesquely named Paradise Island) and were spending part of the winter in their spectacular home. They had expected Sam to arrive somewhat earlier, but our engagement caused a delay of three weeks so that we could fly down with my parents in the Beechcraft. This gave us time to make plans and have more time together. It also gave Marguerite and Axel time to arrange a huge celebration for us which included Sam's Uncle Barret, his cousins Doris and Scott Moxley, Irving Diven and Kitty Robb, as well as Sam's sister, Polly, and her husband, Pete Bassick. They all gathered in Nassau for the celebration, and for once my family was outnumbered.

The fabulous dinner party for fourteen included Marguerite's sister, Gene Gauntier. Axel's launch met us at the Fort Montague Beach Hotel to sail us to the island. It seemed odd to me to take a boat ride when we were fancily dressed in evening clothes, but there was no bridge to the island.

A first meeting with the Wenner-Grens was rather awesome. Marguerite could be charming, coarse and formidable all at the same time. She was a striking woman—tall, big-boned, with dyed black hair and flashing black eyes that penetrated into one's very core. Her personality exuded strength and dominance. Marguerite didn't just dress for dinner, she wore costumes. Flowing gowns of rich velvet or lace, sophisticated and queenly, placed her in center stage. Her jewels were bought as investments and were solid, heavy stones. The necklace she wore for our engagement party had emeralds the size of pigeon eggs, each separated by a great pearl. The heavy strand hung from her shoulders like a lei, as long over her back as over her bosom. From each ear lobe a matching pearl supported a smaller cabachon emerald.

My first personal encounter with her came after dinner when she pulled Sam and me out on the terrace to talk to us alone. She was not happy with Sam's choice of bride. Her aspirations for him took the form of a Swedish blonde or of a certain Nancy Oakes, who lived in Nassau. Nancy was the woman whose husband was accused of murdering her father, Sir Harry Oakes. It was a scandal that burned the tabloids for months, and the trial ended with insufficient proof for conviction, but more than enough for speculation. Nancy was now divorced and living under a spotlight. Sam had never considered her for a moment—in truth, he disliked her—but Marguerite was disappointed to see "her boy" saddled with a widow and two children, thinking they would be an impediment to his career. "Besides, she's too fat," was her spiteful ending. In a small voice, Sam replied, "I like her that way." I was outraged, very angry, and I fully intended not to return the next day for luncheon. In the end, I swallowed my pride for Sam's sake and showed up with the children. Mother and Dad felt I should forgive her rudeness. It was true that she had had too much to drink that evening and that was the last time she vented her spite on me. She was actually cordial and warm from then on. Still, I didn't give her any opportunity to turn on me. She was not one to contradict, and I would not upset Sam's life for anything.

She was really to be pitied. Denied children of her own, she was obviously jealous of women who were more blessed. She lived a lonely life, mostly by choice, rarely accepting invitations. We were honored once by their presence at one of our dinner parties and realized that it was unusual for the couple to leave their home at night.

Marguerite died of alcoholism in 1974, completely alone. She refused to see anyone from the time one of her legs had to be amputated. Her vanity kept her to herself, and the constant phantom pain drove her more and more to the bottle for relief. Axel had died of cancer in 1961, and she never recovered from the grief of losing him. We saw her for the last time in Nassau, shortly after Axel's death and before her circulatory problems began. Her beloved island had been sold to Huntington Hartford, and she was living in a small house near the Fort Montague Beach Hotel.

After an exciting week in Nassau, becoming better acquainted with Sam's family, I flew with Sam to Mexico City to find a house for us. My parents stayed in Nassau with the children.

Another exciting week followed in Mexico City. There I met friends of Sam, who hosted a party for us. We found a suitable house to rent. I then returned regretfully to New York to wait out the remaining ten weeks before our wedding. There was plenty to do. Judy finished her school term at Brearley; I studied Spanish at the Berlitz School, and we packed and moved back to Muncie at the end of May.

Moving was delayed because of chicken pox, brought about by Judy in the first place. Ann was sent promptly to Muncie when Judy broke out with the rash. Nevertheless, Ann and I both came down with the disease on the same day, she in Muncie and I in New York. Immunization shots, immigration papers and passports all had to wait for two weeks until we had recovered. Finally, all was accomplished and we were in Muncie ready for our wedding. It took place on a windy day at our cottage on Lake Maxinkuckee in Culver, Indiana, June 19, 1948.

Our honeymoon was a leisurely drive to Mexico City in my new Buick, a wedding present from Dad. We lived in a furnished apartment at the Latino Americana until my household furniture and goods arrived in September. After our house was in order, my parents flew down in November to bring the children to us. It was wonderful to be together again—a happy reunion. Judy and Ann had reached their seventh and fifth birthdays in the spring of that year. Judy's birthday was celebrated in Nassau and Ann's in Muncie. Sam often said he was happy to have two "ready-made" daughters. Unfortunately, I could not give him a son or another daughter, as I miscarried twice while living in Mexico.

In spite of this, life in Mexico was happy. Sam enjoyed his work at Lecheria Nationale, but we hadn't been long in Mexico City when Axel asked Sam to take over the management of Conquistador, S.A., his silver factory that was not doing well. Sam became so enamored of this creative business that he bought 49% of the stock from Axel and was able to make it the top silver factory in Mexico. Sanburn had a big silver making operation and was a powerful competitor, but Sam's factory made most of the holloware for Taxco, the largest silver center in the country, known by all the tourists. Conquistador was known and respected by silversmiths and tourists alike. Bill Spratling, the famous designer and silversmith, created designs for Conquistador. So did Sam. In 1949, he designed a gorgeous Paul Revere style tea set which won first place in the national silver hollow ware competition in Taxco.

We rented a weekend house in Cuernavaca, which we shared with another couple—first with Kay and Gordon Benedict; then, after the Benedicts moved back to the United States, with Roberta and Ed Sherman. We usually alternated weekends, but sometimes a long holiday would come along. Then we all drove down together and had wonderful restful times—barbecuing our dinners and sitting around the pool, occasionally braving the icy mountain water that filled it.

It was always good to leave the high altitude of Mexico City and bask in the sun of a warmer climate. We kept our closets filled with summer clothes to simplify packing. A caretaker and his wife lived in a little servant house on the property and kept the premises clean, the yard mowed and the flower beds well tended. It was a lovely small house close to the center of town and, like all the houses, surrounded by a high stone wall overflowing with bougainvillea and plumbago vines.

One weekend we arrived to news of a robbery. Two men had climbed over the wall and, at gun point, forced the caretaker to open the house. They then cleaned out our closets. All of Sam's handsome trousers and jackets were gone. I especially grieved for his cherry red linen slacks. He looked so smashing in them when they were topped with a white huayabera shirt. The robbers were particularly interested in men's clothes. Since most of Sam's were new, bought before our wedding, it was a hard loss.

CHAPTER THIRTEEN

After two years of fabulous living in Mexico, Sam's dream of owning his own business became an obsession. If he could find a drug business for sale, he wanted to return to the States. One he had been waiting for was a wholesale company in Kansas City. When he learned it was finally for sale, he flew there to make a bid. He was disappointed to find he was just too late, but he now had the bit in his teeth and began searching for another company. He made several trips to look over available drug companies and, before returning to Mexico City, stopped in Indianapolis to visit with his Uncle Barret.

Barret told him his friend, Keller Brock, was ill and suggested that Sam call on him. Keller owned Haag Drug Company and Sam was glad to visit his old boss. In the course of conversation, Keller learned that Sam was looking for a company to buy. He suggested a look at the Haag chain. Keller intended to retire. By the end of the afternoon, Sam had made Keller an offer which was accepted.

Thus it was that we exchanged our exotic life in Mexico in 1950 for a return to Indianapolis, familiar surroundings and old friends. I laughed when I said that Sam "drug" me back to the States.

When Sam took on the thirty-three stores of the retail drug chain, he had a bear by the tail, but he loved every minute of the hard work. My father had loaned him part of the money to buy the business, but he paid off the loan in a few years. He went on to realize his goal of "making a million" and then set his goal higher.

Sam joined Affiliated Drug, an organization of druggists all over the States. With headquarters in New York, Affiliated was designed to acquaint its members with the latest manufactured items for promotion. Toys, housewares and seasonal merchandise were shown twice a year to the chain store buyers. The executives usually went to the meetings to advise their buyers and to renew friendships with the other members. Sam's creativity and willingness to share his ideas and to accept those of others brought him instant friends and high esteem in the organization. Out of his interest in the business and his innate desire to both teach and learn, he developed a program for exchange of ideas among the retail druggists which he called "What's Good With You." The sessions stimulated new ideas for sales, management, publicity and all facets of running profitable stores. He became an officer in Affiliated and later was president for a few years.

Sam had an original idea of computer control over inventory. He started this with an early IBM machine. This set the ball rolling with other chains around the country after they learned of the success at Haag. Most of this inventory control method was developed while we were on a cruise to Rio and Buenos Aires in 1959. During the month at sea, going and coming back, Sam spent every morning in the quiet of the ship's library, able to work out his concept without interruption—something that would have been impossible in his office at Haag. In spite of opposition and derision from other executives, Sam persevered, bought the 1060 computer and set the inventory control method rolling. His concept was so sound that IBM later incorporated much of his thinking and methodology into their famous Impact System, which was the yardstick of inventory control for nearly two decades. The introduction of the computer system reduced Haag's inventory by one million dollars and enabled the company to add four new stores.

My brother, Bill, who had worked for Sam at Conquistador to gain experience in business management, also worked at Haag when we returned to Indianapolis. In 1951 Sam sent Bill to Los Angeles to work for Rexall Drug Company in order to learn their self-serve system. Businesses were just beginning to adopt self-service, and Sam wanted a report on how successful it was in drug stores. Bill took his meals in a nearby Huddle Restaurant and was impressed by its obvious popularity. The place was always full of customers because the food and service were excellent, the prices reasonable and the atmosphere congenial. Bill thought this type of restaurant was the answer to the outmoded drug store soda fountains, which were becoming unprofitable. Bill phoned Sam and asked him to come to Los Angeles. Sam caught Bill's enthusiasm and flew out to see for himself. Bill had had a stunning brainstorm for Haag. Paul Cummins, the owner of The Huddle, agreed to sell the rights to Haag for $1200. Haag could use its name, menu and decor—in short create duplicates of the one in Los Angeles. The Huddle Restaurants were the first of their kind to replace the drug store soda fountain. They were run as a separate business, but adjoined the drug stores. More and more of these attractive restaurants were added as larger Haag stores were built in shopping centers around Indiana and Ohio. They became popular and fashionable gathering places. My brother's find netted Haag a huge profit. Later, Bill bought the chain and ran the restaurants on his own. The installation of the Huddles was so unique and revolutionary that a representative of Rexall came to Indianapolis from Los Angeles to copy the idea for their stores—even though the original Huddle was only three blocks from his store!

In 1955 Sam had built what was at that time the largest drug store east of the Mississippi and that first Huddle Restaurant had adjoined it. It was constructed at 56th and Illinois and opened with a celebration to match its size, a block long and half-a-block wide. The opening featured a trained elephant, rented for the occasion, to do tricks and attract a crowd. Klieg lights at night, banners and news ads did the rest. The place was mobbed. Balloons and souvenirs were given out with the sales, and business boomed. Merchandise heretofore unheard of in drug stores, such as picket fencing and power mowers, was offered for sale.

The elephant gave Haag more publicity than it bargained for. It was for sale at a "cut-rate" price of $999.99 (cut down from $1000). A jeweler, seeking publicity for his establishment, offered to "buy" the elephant and arrived at the parking lot with news photographers to flash him as he presented his check to Sam. Unfortunately, he never cashed in on more publicity, but Haag did. The trainer left with the elephant, but never arrived at the jewelry store. Two days later, the elephant was found, abandoned and trumpeting with hunger, in the truck on a side road. The trainer had skipped with Sam's check and disappeared.

The aftermath of the elephant's visit caused Haag large problems. There was the matter of clean-up. A considerable pile of elephant refuse needed to be hauled away. The city would not collect it unless it was bagged. Sam thought of selling it off to customers as "great rose manure," but there wasn't time as the entire area began to give off a scent that drove customers away. After the emergency bagging effort, the city still refused to haul it away and required Haag to truck it off and bury it beyond the city limits.

Mother, a passionate animal lover who bred and raised numerous pets, bemoaned the fate of the elephant. "If only there had been two, I would have bought them," she said, adding, "I only buy in pairs."

Sam built the chain up to fifty-seven stores, counting a seventeen store chain that he bought from the Jacob Drug Company in Atlanta. After the merger he brought several key people to Indianapolis from Atlanta. One of these was Jim Steele, who was first treasurer of the company and then president after Sam's semi-retirement in 1967. At that time Sam became chairman of the board, which position he held until 1972 when he retired completely.

Sam had many opportunities to sell the chain, but he backed away from those who might change the entire operation and fire most of his employees. He felt a great loyalty towards all his personnel and refused to allow another organization to put anyone out of work because of his need to retire. One of the bidders for Haag was George Roberts of Bear Sterns in New York. Roberts became famous as part of K.K.R. (Kravis, Kolberg, Roberts), possibly the world's best known buy-out firm. In his desire to keep ownership within his own "family," Sam conceived the idea of selling to his own executives. This leveraged buy-out was a fascinating part of American business long before L.B.O.s became famous on Wall Street and at Harvard.

Haag was sold to five of Sam's junior executives. They ran the company extremely well, expanding the chain to other states and operating about seventy-five stores. The success of the business only intensified the desire of larger firms to take it over. Unfortunately, a Chicago partner, owning seventy-five percent of the stock, decided he wanted his money for another investment. He sold Haag Drug Company to Peoples Drug of Washington D.C. in 1979.

After Sam retired, he joined the Society of Retired Executives and participated enthusiastically in their projects. He worked as a consultant on the Small Business Committee, giving help and advice to those wanting to start a business, to students looking for their special field of work, or to small businesses in trouble. He gave many hours to S.R.E. and supported it with donations.

Sam's aim in life was to contribute what he could to others, particularly his family and those he loved. He was touched by people who were ambitious, but who lacked the means or the knowledge to further their careers. So, he gave freely of advice and/or dollars to members of his family—nieces and nephews, cousins, in-laws and grandchildren, as well as to his mother and sister and my daughters. His thoughtfulness extended to friends and charitable organizations. He was on the mailing list of every "give me, buy me or try me" appeal imaginable.

Sam worked hard all his life to create a future that he could enjoy. His early savings, pinching pennies for investments, building and earning, and taking few risks paid off. Underneath his softness was a man who was intolerant of wasted intelligence, immoral living, and sloth. His judgment of an individual was usually accurate.

He was wonderful company at parties. He remembered jokes to the letter and regaled his listeners with hilarious stories. Sometimes he monopolized the conversation if he was engrossed in the subject. My brother once commented that if you asked Sam what time it was, he told you how to make a watch.

Many of Sam's ideas proved important for progress. One was forecasting fluctuations of the stock market on the computer. Not having time to do the work himself, he asked Anacomp, a consulting firm, to study the market and send him reports of the action. Anacomp was not interested in taking on such a time consuming project, but a young man working part time for the firm, Nicholas Kaiser, asked if he could devote his time to the research. Nick was then in the army, stationed at Fort Benjamin Harrison. As soon as Sam and Nick met, their minds fell into place together. Sam gave Nick his experiments to work out on the Haag office computer during the hours the machine was not in use. Often Nick worked late into the night trying different studies on transaction tapes bought from the New York Stock Exchange. Nick sorted out the data on about fifteen hundred selected stocks from the extraneous garbage on the daily transactions to make his analysis. After months of analyzing stock trends, Nick developed a computer program which would inform the buyer when to buy or sell an identified stock. In testing the program, Sam selected a few stocks and compared the forecast with Wall Street activities. Sometimes they were in agreement, but often the computer went against the trends—only to win in the long run.

Nick and Sam formed a little partnership company they called Odds (Optimal Digital Decisions Systems) which soon expanded as the program was successful. Martin Zweig was one who bought reports from Odds to start his forecasting operation in the east.

Unified Management was a small, troubled company which Nick and Sam bought and merged Odds into the operation. Nick built Unified Management into a major business management firm and, in a few years, had customers all over the United States, handling over five hundred million dollars for investments in stocks, bonds and mutual funds.

This enterprise, beginning with a small seed—"a game to play with a computer"—netted Sam three million dollars when the company was sold to Mony in the '80s.

Sharing the cake at our wedding, June 19, 1948, Culver, Indiana. My daughter, Ann, age five, a flower girl with her sister Judy (not pictured).

On the pier at the wedding reception (l to r) R. Bill Diven, Irving Moxley Diven, David Moxley, Doris Moxley, Scott Moxley.

A pre-wedding party. David Moxley; Agnes Ball (Lucina's mother); Barret Moxley, Scott Moxley, William Ball (Lucina's father): Doris Moxley (Note reflection of David in the mirror).

The winter vacation home of the Axel Wenner-Grens on Paradise Island, Nassau, Bahamas. It was called Hog Island when Axel owned it in 1948.

Axel and Marguerite greeting King Gustav of Sweden.

Top and left: Marguerite Wenner-Gren with her pet monkey and chihuahuas. Center: Wenner-Gren's city home, 390 Paseo de la Reforma, Mexico City.

The dining room at Ranch Cortez, Cuernavaca.

649 Sierra Amatepec, Mexico City. A view of our home—1948-1950.

Example of silver pattern made by Conquistador, S.A., Sam's silver factory in Mexico, which he owned in partnership with Axel Wenner-Gren.

4106 Washington Blvd, Indianapolis, Indiana. Our home from 1950-1960.

Sam on Scott Moxley's motorcycle.

Wedding day for Irving and Frank Springer.

Sam at an Affiliated Drug convention, New York—1954.

Sam c. 1960.

11612 Williams Creek Drive, Carmel, Indiana. Our home from 1960-1989.

Today in Business

Haag's Buys 17-Store Chain

By Harold Hartley

IF ANYONE has been watching the heels of Sam Moxley they can see he has been kicking up quite a bit of dust.

He is president of the Haag drug chain which has been booming.

I met him at a board meeting a few days ago. He had a little slip of paper in his pocket. Sam was happy, mighty happy.

Haag's sales last year took off like a missile. Bigger stores, aggressive merchandising, advertising did the trick. All these plus Sam's own sleeves-up work.

At the last annual board meeting Haag's split its stock two-for-one. But this is just the beginning.

HAAG'S NOW has acquired a 17-store drug chain in the Atalnta, Ga., area. The Jacobs Pharmacy Co. will become a wholly owned subsidiary.

Sam Moxley will keep all of the employees in this leading drug firm in the South.

In his mild way he said this is just a part of Haag's multi-million dollar expansion program planned for the next 15 months.

Sam (it's Sampson B.) said Haag's has tripled its sales in the last six years.

THIS YEAR he is spending more than a million dollars on new stores in Indiana.

The chain now has 47 stores, including 29 in Central Indiana, and one in Hamilton, O.

There is no limit to the vision of Sampson B. Moxley, who is taking his success like a trouper, and still cuts his own lawn.

A glowing article about Sam and Haag Drug Co. written by Harold Hartley, in *The Indianapolis Times*, c. 1950-59.

Office of the Mayor · City of Indianapolis

City of Indianapolis

Hereby Gratefully Acknowledges The Outstanding Services Of

SAM B. MOXLEY

Whose Contribution Toward The Betterment Of The Community Has Been Conspicuously Demonstrated In The Role Of

MEMBER

INDIANAPOLIS EMPLOYMENT & TRAINING ADVISORY COUNCIL

1975 - 1978

William H. Hudnut

MARCH 2, 1978

Mayor Hudnut's proclamation to Sam for outstanding community service, 1978.

CHAPTER FOURTEEN

In 1967 Sam began having health problems which led to his gradual retirement from business. The Cleveland Clinic discovered from heart catheterization that he had scar tissue on his heart. This caused a bundle branch block and a lazy AV node, resulting in an irregular, weak heart beat. He was told not to swim or exercise strenuously. He could walk, but not jog. This suited Sam very well as he preferred his bed to a chair and spent longer and longer hours resting. His circulation was poor, his blood pressure high, and his medication kept increasing.

Sam loved to cook and after his full retirement in 1972, he took over the kitchen duties and grocery shopping, while I spent those hours teaching or practicing. My two-piano partner and I gave many programs and worked diligently together to improve our ensemble. Sam served his and my dinners on trays and we ate in bed, watching the news and our favorite T.V. shows. I served Sam his breakfast in bed. Sam loved gourmet food and exotic foreign recipes and produced many wonderful dishes for our dinners. He tried to keep us on low-salt, low-fat meals, but somehow his love for hollandaise sauce, lobster tails and steak interfered with the low cholesterol diet he tried to maintain. The results showed on both our waistlines.

Finally, he was eating all his meals in bed with a T.V. accompaniment. By 1983, he had gone through two by-pass surgeries on his left leg and been faced with a threat of amputation when circulation stopped because of a blocked artery. He was not deterred or discouraged by his medical problems, even when he fought bladder tumors for five years. Each year he had an operation to remove them. Finally radiation stopped the malignant growths which chemo-therapy had failed to cure.

1985 was a sad year for both of us. Sam's mother, Leona, had a stroke on Christmas Day, 1984, and though it seemed at first she might recover, days stretched into months of gradual debilitation. She was bedfast for eleven months before relinquishing her life at ninety-eight the following November.

After her stroke, Sam and I used the house in Naples, Florida, which she had rented for February and March. For a decade we had shared vacations there with Leona. Sam would drive her down on the first of February and cook and care for her. I followed on the first of March. I couldn't be away two full months because of my teaching schedule. I also did not like to leave the house vulnerable to a furnace malfunction and possible freezing pipes. With Leona unable to travel, but with a lease signed and deposits made, Sam and I decided to use the house for just one month.

We were enjoying our time there until calls came from my daughter, Judy, alerting us to my mother's declining health. Mother had brooded constantly over the loss of Dad in 1980 and no longer had the will to live without him. Now, five years later at age ninety-three, she simply went to bed, turned her thoughts inward and prepared to die.

Alarmed, I insisted we start for home immediately. We packed and were quickly on our way. Three days later we arrived home, but by that time Mother could hardly communicate. It was possible she was having a series of small strokes, but she refused to go to the hospital. I hired a nurse for her and called a doctor-friend, who agreed to see her at home every day. It was obvious Mother would not recover even with intravenous feeding and drugs. Her kidneys failed and she slipped peacefully away on March fifth, one week after we got home.

We both lost our mothers, just a few months apart. Sam grieved more quietly than I did, but just as deeply. The ties to one's mother are strong. When they are broken it is like another umbilical cord wrenched away.

The three years from 1985 to 1988 were ones of heavy travel. No sooner did we return from one trip than we were off on another. Sam's failing health made him determined to do as much as possible before it was too late. Although he did not discuss his fears with me, I knew he was afraid he would have to face further surgery on his leg and probably have an amputation. My fears of being caught far from home and help were ever-present, but I could not insist we remain at home. I tried to steer him to trips where we could get medical attention in a hurry, but this was not possible every time. On those trips I worried constantly. I felt I was sitting on a time bomb. When explosions did come, they happened in the worst possible places.

❦

My Christmas gifts from Sam in 1987 were two soirées planned for early winter. The parties would be elegant in each case, with a catered buffet dinner following a piano recital. The first occasion was to feature Ruth Slenczynska on Sunday, January 17th, the second, James Tocco on February 14, 1988.

Before we left on a cruise in November, we made arrangements with the caterer and with each artist. I was thrilled to be able to host two of my favorite artists, who were also good friends, and I looked forward to a busy time at the beginning of the new year.

We flew to Rio for a few quiet days before boarding the Royal Viking Sea which was scheduled to cruise up the Amazon River and back through the Carribean Islands, winding up in Fort Lauderdale. We would be home after Christmas, but before the New Year.

The five days spent in Rio were a lazy loaf in and around the hotel on Ipanema Beach. We cased the jewelry shops and fell victim to the wiles of supersalesmanship. Sam bought an emerald for Ann and an aquamarine for Judy, their birthstones. He also found a beautiful amethyst ring and earrings for me, all lovely and expensive.

We boarded the ship on November 30 and found our familiar stateroom on the Atlantic deck, where we had berthed before on the sister ship, Royal Viking Sky. The ships are much the same, luxurious with a friendly crew.

The second night at sea Sam was awake all night with intense cramping in his left leg—the same one that had undergone two by-passes and was nearly amputated each time. His surgeon had warned him that he would not be able to save the leg a third time. Now he was facing another circulation block.

The ship's doctor advised us to disembark at Belem, the next port, and try to reach home before a complete blockage occurred. We made air reservations back to Rio and Miami and were ready to leave the ship three days later. In the meantime, since Sam could not walk without pain, he was given a wheel chair, and I wheeled him around the ship and to the dining room for meals. We played duplicate bridge in the afternoons and attended the bridge lectures, thus managing to enjoy a little of the cruise and to meet other passengers. Two couples at our table during meals were particularly congenial. One couple, Polly and Jim Patterson, who were near our own ages, became real friends.

We were very worried. The doctor checked the pulse in Sam's leg every day. He seemed not to be worsening, but at any time a complete blockage could occur which would necessitate immediate surgery. We were so far from help! If circulation did stop before we reached Rio, surgery would have to be done there. We could only hope that his condition would remain stable at least until we arrived in Miami. It was a nerve-wracking journey. In Belem we waited four hours for our plane to arrive. We feared missing our connection in Rio and began negotiations for a charter plane. Just then the commuter plane arrived and we took off promptly. Even so the connection in Rio was so tight that without Sam in a wheel chair we could not have made it. We were told at the gate that we could not board as our baggage had not yet been transferred. Again, at the last second our bags got on board and we were allowed to leave.

The all-night flight brought us to Miami at six a.m. The sleepy airport was all but shut down except for the Delta counter, but there was a flight for Indianapolis at eight a.m. I bought our tickets and we were home by noon and on the telephone to Sam's surgeon.

Three days later on December 6, successful surgery was performed. Sam did not lose his leg. Instead of the artificial arteries that had been used before, a vein was taken from his right leg to insert into the left. The doctor was not concerned about the possibility of amputation. He explained that much progress had been made in surgical techniques over the past four years. Though the two surgeons who had operated on Sam previously felt Sam's veins were not serviceable ("rotten" was the word they used), the veins seemed adequate this time.

In spite of the successful surgery, Sam suffered severe after effects. His kidneys failed and he developed an incredibly painful case of pseudo-gout, an inflamation which paralyzed his hands, shoulders and neck in a daily progression. He looked like death and lost twenty-five pounds almost overnight. His condition was critical. I became thoroughly alarmed.

Judy and Ann had arrived to spend Christmas with us, Judy from Cape Cod and Ann from Boulder, Colorado. They too were frightened. Sam was finally released on Christmas Eve, but it was the most depressing Christmas I can remember. Our efforts to make the day festive fell flat as he was unable to eat or even sit at the table. Sam was so thin his skin hung like draperies on his body. The open wound at the groin on his right leg, where the incision was made to remove the vein, needed dressing twice a day. It was a nasty looking hole that had become infected.

The kidney malfunction had weakened and dehydrated Sam so alarmingly that I took him back to the hospital on New Year's Day. I was terribly frightened, but intravenous fluids revived him and he finally began to mend. I thought the party in January should be cancelled, but Sam insisted the plans remain in place. He was sure he would be strong enough by January seventeenth. I mailed the invitations after extracting a promise that he would rest in bed from time to time that evening if he didn't feel well. He agreed, and the party went on as scheduled. Ruth and her husband, James Kerr, arrived Friday evening with plenty of time for her to rest and practice before Sunday afternoon.

Ruth had never played so beautifully. Our guests outdid themselves with applause and a standing ovation, which she graciously acknowledged with exciting encores. The entire evening was a great success, topped by an extravagantly gorgeous display of flowers placed on a pedestal between the two Hamburg Steinways. The flowers were a gift for the event from Sam's cousin, Irving Springer, and her husband, Frank. Sam, exhausted by the effort of playing host, did escape to the bedroom to rest several times during the evening.

Just before Christmas, I had received a call from Mrs. Tocco. She reported that Jim had returned from Europe with serious eye trouble. He had been told to cancel all engagements for six months as he was in danger of losing his sight. At that time, Sam was still in the hospital. We knew he was facing another operation for an aneurism. I felt we had excellent reasons for cancelling the recital party scheduled for February. Sam, however, was terribly let down at the prospect. He suggested that I call Pia Sebastiani in Muncie to ask her to do the program. Luckily, she had just returned from Argentina and she graciously agreed to play. I was delighted. She is a brilliant pianist and also a good friend.

The Valentine party was just as delightful as the one in January. We entertained a different group of friends. The decorations were all hearts and flowers. We again had a splendid bouquet to place between the pianos and create a festive stage.

Sam was still not up to par and retired often to the bedroom. The guests understood, of course, and, with plenty of help in the kitchen, I was able to double as host and hostess. Pia played a beautiful program. The crowd loved her. The double Christmas gift of two soirées went off without a hitch in spite of the trips to the hospital and all the worry and concern. Sam's legs were wobbly, but he was game and pushing.

His next operation fell on March sixth, three months to the day after his by-pass. X-rays had disclosed a dangerous aneurism, ballooning below the renal artery. There were also three smaller ones beginning to swell into each iliac artery. The incision cut across his abdomen from hip to hip. He had no recurring kidney problems, but he had a terrible time regaining his strength. He suffered chest pains along with nausea and vomiting. In April, he went back to the hospital for a heart catheterization. This time he got a good report. His arteries appeared clear and the pains were called "spasms of the lower esophagus." He was to take a nitrostat at the onset of pain. These stopped the pain almost at once.

For some time Sam had also suffered from congestive heart failure. Often during the night he was short of breath. When he was lying down, his heart could not pump the fluid from his lungs. Sam was hospitalized part of every month from December to May, but he did achieve control over the fluid build-up in his lungs with the use of a diuretic.

I have described these physical problems of Sam's to show how courageous and stubborn he was in his determination to continue the life-style he so enjoyed. He wanted to travel and enjoy life as long as possible before he was "on crutches." He said more than once, "I would rather die somewhere abroad than sit in an easy chair vegetating at home." We were both well aware of his precarious health. I understood him, even though I did not altogether agree. I just wanted to have him with me as long as possible.

Even after the long winter of illness and surgery, Sam was still determined not to cancel the summer travel we had arranged the year before. I was apprehensive about so many trips so close together, particularly the tour of Russia scheduled for September, but Sam announced with a grin that if I didn't want to go, he would find somebody else to go with him.

The first trip, to Scotland and England, began on June eighteenth. It was conducted by the curator of the Indianapolis Museum of Art, Ian Fraser. A Scot himself, Ian was impressively knowledgeable about his country and the museums we visited.

The flight on TWA was miserable—rough, cold food, poor service and a thoroughly uncomfortable, sleepless night. It was bad planning to take us to London when the tour was to begin in Glasgow. At dawn in Heathrow Airport, we found ourselves in a seething mass of humanity. It was oppressively hot. After an exhausting delay and an effort to change planes, we finally reached Glasgow, burned out by the long flights.

There was a party to welcome us that evening, hosted by the tour group from the museum. It was our fortieth wedding anniversary. We were toasted with champagne, given gifts and a special cake for dessert. Two other couples turned out to be celebrating their fortieth also. It was a curious coincidence which made the party joyous.

Forty years of marriage is properly marked with gifts of rubies. I had gold cuff links made for Sam, with a strip of small rubies lining the side of each link. He gave me a pair of ruby earrings circled with diamonds, but when I put them on he realized they were too small and unbecoming. He then sketched a backing for them to be made in gold and took the earrings back to the jeweler. The round frame enlarged the earrings to cover my ear lobes and set off the rubies. They were to be ready on our return from Russia in September.

The highlight of our three days in Glasgow was a visit to the Burrell Collection, which Burrell had donated to the city. A splendid building housed this private collection of many art styles preceding the Impressionistic Period. A breathtaking collection, it is the largest and most important ever donated to a city.

Our bus took us to Edinburgh where we spent three days touring the environs and the castles. Ian escorted us to Newbattle Abbey, his grandfather's home. Ian spent his early childhood in the castle-like edifice on acres of rolling ground amid enormous old trees. Newbattle Abbey, a school for adults, was begun by Ian's grandfather and was still in operation. Ian proved to be an excellent guide. We visited many places we would not have been able to see without him.

On our way to London, we stopped for tea at the home of some friends of his near Edinburgh. Their house was at the edge of a lake in a small village. The rooms were jammed with beautiful antiques and the dining table was loaded with high tea goodies. Our group of fifty filled the small rooms to overflowing with laughter and conviviality.

We left Scotland and drove on to York for the night. That evening we made a surprise visit to Castle Howard, the most glamorous event of the entire trip. We arrived before dark in time to tour the magnificent castle, privately owned by the Howard family since its construction in the early 1700s. To raise funds for repairs and regular maintenance, elegant dinners are served. The popularity of these functions is so great that reservations must be made a year in advance.

The grounds are extensive, planted with a beautiful rose garden and populated with strutting peacocks, who perched on the stone verandas and pierced the darkening air with their cacophonous shrieks.

When we arrived, we were ushered into ancient pews in the chapel for an organ recital—a wonderful way to set the stage for a truly memorable evening. We admired the splendid altar, the Corinthian pillars and the golden glow cast through the stained glass windows onto the cherry wood of the pews.

Each room and passageway in the castle was furnished with great taste and elegance. Fabulous porcelains and tapestries added to the sumptuousness of the decor. Our tour ended in the Great Hall, where a roaring fire in an immense fireplace took the chill out of the night air. Champagne and hors d'oeuvres were served by waiters in black tie evening clothes and waitresses in black dresses with white aprons and tiny white caps.

After cocktails we were led through the long passages and down the marble staircase to the Garden Room, our banquet hall. We sat at round tables for eight, set with crystal, silver glistening on white tablecloths and softly lit with pink candles. The ladies received favors and corsages presented on silver trays. During the gourmet dinner we were entertained with dinner music, performed by the organist (now turned pianist) and a violinist. Both were versatile, expert musicians. The potpourri of selections covered all types and periods of music—ballads, Strauss waltzes and selections from musicals and opera, ranging from Mozart to Mancini. The wonderful evening was crowned by a full moon as we boarded the bus for the late ride back to York. We felt as though we had truly been regaled by royalty.

Our last three days in London were spent visiting museums, but the best time Sam and I had was an evening alone together at the musical, *Les Miserables*, a splendid production of Victor Hugo's novel, faithfully depicted and magnificently acted.

We had thought the tour might be too strenuous for Sam, but he managed very well. He paced himself and was able to walk almost as much as everyone else. We liked the members of the group and made new friends. Altogether, the trip was very pleasant. Our close friends, Dottie and Wayne Ritter were along, and it was fun to be with them.

We spent the month of July at home. I resumed teaching while Sam rested and worked at his desk. By early August, we were ready for our Alaskan cruise on the Royal Viking Star leaving from Vancouver. This was our credit cruise—the choice we were given after having to abort the Amazon River cruise in December. We had cruised the Inland Passage years before, taking along Ann and her children, Tracey, aged ten, and Bryan, aged seven. We remembered the beauty of the scenery and how pleasant the voyage had been, so we chose it as an easy trip, one where Sam could rest when he chose or take part in the ship's tours, activities, and entertainment, if he wished.

It was a good cruise. Sam gained weight with the abundant food, and, of course, so did I. The weather was good most of the time. We enjoyed the salmon bakes on shore while watching the Indian dances. Sitka gave us a glimpse of old Russia, where we would be within the month. We resisted buying souvenirs, knowing we would find the same things in the Beriozka shops in Russia later on.

We arrived in San Francisco, relaxed and rested and had two nostalgic days at the St. Francis Hotel on Union Square—our favorite spot on the west coast. Trader Vic's for dinner was a must, and we couldn't leave the city without browsing through Gump's famous department store.

Polly and Jim Patterson, our dinner companions on the Royal Viking Sea in December, drove in from Mill Valley and took us to their home for dinner. We renewed our acquaintance and became good friends over drinks and good food. The Pattersons, easy to talk to and nice to be with, tentatively planned a trip with us in the future. Sam had already arranged for a Tauck Tour to New Orleans in November, combining a tour through Cajun country with a cruise on the Mississippi Queen, but they couldn't join us for this one.

We were home for only two weeks before leaving for Russia. My apprehension was softened by the knowledge that Judy and Ann would be with us. I still worried about the long flights and the stress of sightseeing for Sam. I was chilled at the thought of being behind the Iron Curtain in hostile territory, even though tensions had eased somewhat with Gorbachev's new policies of Glasnost and Perestroika.

CHAPTER FIFTEEN

September second was our departure date. We flew to Logan Airport in Boston and arrived ahead of Ann's flight from Denver. She was surprised and delighted to see us as she walked off the plane. Then we were off to find Judy, who would be coming in from the Cape by bus. Soon we were four. Breathless from walking and toting our carry-on bags, we joined the assemblage of our tour group at the Lufthansa gate for the overnight flight to Frankfort. By ones, twos and threes we met our new travel companions. It was an Alumni Holiday tour with the seventy-eight alumni divided between Dartmouth and Brown Universities. Since Judy was an alumna from Pembroke (coördinate college with Brown University), she received brochures and information on their trips with Alumni Holiday. We were able to go with her as family members. We were pleased to see one gentleman, Dan Tolman, who had traveled with us before on the Alumni Holiday tour to Australia and New Zealand in 1987. Judy and Ann were among the youngest in the group, most of the others being closer to our ages.

The Lufthansa flight was pleasanter than the TWA to Scotland, but the cramped quarters and long hours left us exhausted on arrival in Frankfort. We were given rooms in the Sheraton Airport Hotel and sank thankfully into bed for six hours.

A wake-up call brought us all to the alert, and we gathered again for another Lufthansa plane to carry us on to Leningrad.

As we sank towards the city in preparation for landing, I peered out the window to see acres of white buildings, all the same height and nearly the same size lining the streets like a huge prison compound. They appeared uncompromising and cold.

When we drove through those streets, however, I discovered that the buildings, though all trimmed in white, were painted in various pastel colors. Shades of yellow, pink, green or blue made them quite attractive. The avenues were wide with colorful flower beds lining each side. Trees were plentiful, and monuments or statues were prominent on almost every corner. There were no cars to speak of and almost no people. It seemed like an abandoned city.

We finally found one populated street, the long Nevsky Prospekt, where most shops and movie houses were located. This broad avenue was jammed with people standing in line to enter the cinema.

We were driven to our hotel on the outskirts of town, an enormous hunk of concrete, twelve stories high, with its impressive Russian title, *Pribaltiuskaya*, printed across the entire roof line. But the inner city of Leningrad, the rule of not more than five stories on any building has held fast since the time of Peter the Great. Peter built the city, then called Saint Petersburg, on a swampy marsh beside the Neva River. The project was considered impossible—a madman's dream, but at the cost of many lives it was finally completed. Summers there are hot and humid, winters so cold the Neva River freezes solid. For months navigation takes place in sledges.

Our group was assigned two large Intourist buses, with a guide for each bus. They would be with us throughout the two-week tour to translate, see to our needs and lecture, both aboard the buses and in the museums. Coincidentally, our guides happened to have the same name—Marina—but that was the only similarity between them. Marina One was short, vivacious and ever-smiling. Her thick, dark hair was massed fluffily on her head and hung to her shoulders. She dressed smartly, and anything she wore complimented her fresh complexion and snappy brown eyes. Her English was perfect, her manners were delightful. We were immediately drawn to Marina One.

Marina Two was also attractive and a good guide, but lacked warmth and friendliness. She had a rather severe demeanor and wore a serious, sometimes cross, expression on her round, Russian countenance. The girls were attached to buses marked "One" and "Two." We had to choose one and then remain on it for the day so the guides could keep track of us. Our two directors were both English. Philip Ryan was Number One and Gary Smith was Number Two. We switched back and forth each day to hear the different viewpoints of our leaders. Peter was knowledgeable and led the group expertly. Gary provided dry wit and comic relief.

Two professors, one from Dartmouth and one from Brown, were excellent lecturers—tops in their fields of Russian history and politics. Each one gave three lectures on the tour, taking turns in the different cities we visited. At each stop one of them would talk about the history, culture and politics of the locality. The lectures added interest and provided insight into the country.

During the summer, we had received books on various aspects of Russian government, history and culture. They were heavy reading, so Sam and I divided them and gave each other book reports to save time. We felt the reading beforehand broadened our understanding.

More than anything else, I had looked forward to seeing the famous Hermitage with its collection of art treasures, but it turned out to be disappointing. Thirty-five thousand people go through the Hermitage every day, and we were there on Sunday, the most popular day of the week. The place was swarming with humanity in ninety-five degree heat. Our Marina One made us stick to her like glue because it would have been easy to get lost and be unable to find our way out of the maze of rooms. We "saw" one picture in each room. We couldn't see more before we were whisked into another. We dashed past fabulous Rembrandts with scarcely a glance. Paintings were so poorly lit that one had to get close to read the titles and the painter's names. It was impossible to see more than a fraction of the collection, the place was so vast.

The two hours spent in the Hermitage made me grieve for the life of those treasures. Polluted by the breath of millions, subjected to the humidity, intense summer heat and intense winter cold with no temperature control in the building, there is a question of how many more years the art will last. Peeling and flaking is apparent in many of the paintings, which cry out for restoration.

Sam was smart. He took off by himself, to the chagrin of Marina, and spent his time with the Impressionist paintings on the top floor, where we ended the tour. All that time I was afraid he was lost.

The most exciting day was the excursion to Petrodvorets, the summer palace of Peter the Great, set on a beautiful island. Sam was not able to walk very far. His legs would begin to ache, and his arthritic hip gave him a lot of pain. He chose to ride the bus across the bridge to the island, but most of the rest of us travelled by hydrofoil across the Baltic. A fleet of these boats were used for excursions. They propelled us past the city's dense grove of businesses into a region where the banks on either side of the Neva River flourished with green, lush foliage.

We docked at a pier a considerable distance from the palace, but what a chance to view it on the approach! On the left of the walkway, a long channel of water led to the distant palace on top of a hill. At its base golden statuary towered up from a large pond spewing fountains of water. Massive staircases on either side led to the top where the palace stood. Beside the staircases, cascades of water plunged to the pool. The palace, with its belvedere, was painted a deep golden yellow trimmed with white. It was aloof and stately.

As we approached the palace, swans idled snobbily among the water plants in the canal. To our right, a forest of superb old trees with inviting paths tempted exploration. Begonias in full color lined the pathway, which was interspersed with statues of golden gods and godesses. I felt I was approaching the fairy tale castle of

Sleeping Beauty. The scene was so regal and entrancing that thrills coursed down my spine.

We were breathless from walking up the steep steps. Looking back towards the way we had come, we saw the spectacular view from the belvedere of the fountains playing below, cascades of water spilling down the sides of the staircase and the gold statues, in attitudes of abandon, playing in the fountains. Far in the distance was the dock where we had landed—the same dock where Peter had disembarked, no doubt met by a carriage or his favorite horse for a ride to the palace.

This was the island occupied by the Germans during the four-year siege of Leningrad during World War II. They had been relentless in their efforts to burn, bomb and starve out the city and would have succeeded but for the intervention of the United States. The Germans desecrated the island, felled hundreds of ancient trees and, when they departed, bombed the palace into near ruin.

It has been an enormous task to restore the palace and grounds to their original condition. So far, restoration has cost 450 million rubles, and only one-third of the palace has been renovated. Even so, there were many rooms to see, far more elegant than any I have visited in Europe. Wallpaper, upholstery and draperies had been duplicated to match the original decor. The furnishings, paintings and collections of porcelain were superb.

After three nights in Leningrad, seeing the magnificent spectacle of St. Isaac's Cathedral, the imposing fortress built to guard the city and house both the army and its prisoners, and the church where the Tsars and their families were entombed, we flew to Tbilisi, the capital of Georgia, close to the border of Turkey.

Georgia is a beautiful country with mountains and fertile plains skirting the coast of the Black Sea. The climate is tropical and produces tea, fruits and vegetables for most of the Soviet Union. Ancient villages and picturesque landscapes beguile the tourists, and the people are the friendliest and most hospitable of any in that part of the world. They are also industrious and proud. Often a stranger will be approached and invited home for tea or supper. Once there, the visitor is treated to all the best the family has to offer, even if that means the family will have little to eat for the next few days.

Our flight to Tbilisi was our first Aeroflot experience. As we boarded the crowded Russian airplane, searching for unreserved seats, the aisle felt like a springboard, so feeble was the construction of the plane. Seat cushions were torn and dirty—some not even on steel frames. They served as flotation cushions as well and looked as if they had already had ditching use. Some of the seat belts were broken or nonexistent. In flight a small cup of water was passed. Russians drink a mineral water, gaseous and yellow, which I found undrinkable. We were warned not to use the lavatory, as unspeakable conditions lurked within. The aroma filtering through the cabin confirmed this. The flight was a long five hours and so noisy that conversation was impossible, because the planes have no mufflers to quiet the motor noise. They sound like army jets taking off.

We approached Tbilisi after dark and the city lights below winked in welcome. The pilot attempted several landings, rising again and again to circle the city. After a half-hour of fingernail biting, we finally landed, and our thoroughly frightened group gratefully deplaned.

Rain and wind drove hard against us as we waited for conveyances to take us to the tour buses. They had been waiting for our arrival for over an hour. Drenched, we found seats and met our two new guides. Strangely, both of them also shared the same name. Two Lollis joined our two Marinas.

We were driven to our hotel. Our tour director, Philip Ryan, had been right when he said the hotel in Leningrad was the best on the tour and the one in Tbilisi the worst. The whole building was run-down. Our "chambre" was tiny, threadbare and none too clean. The bathroom was a box, and the shower had no curtain. The towels were insignificant, none matching in texture or color. We used the only chair and the little floor space for our bags, which we lived out of since there was no hanging space.

Ann was quite sick and running a fever. She stayed in bed the next day after we insisted she see the hotel doctor. Marina One escorted us to the doctor's office where Ann was glanced over and given an antibiotic. She was desperate for tissues as hers had long been used up. The doctor gave her a package of sterile gauze cloths, since there are no tissues in Russia. I gave her the roll of toilet paper we had been advised to bring along since the Russian type is poor-quality-slick. These emergency rations had to do, but as the germs spread to Judy and then to Sam our supplies dwindled. Coughing, blowing and burning with fever, my family stayed in bed instead of sightseeing. There was no such thing as room service, but dear Marina One brought bowls of soup or tea to the girls several times. I sneaked what I could from the table to take to Sam. He was not bedfast until we arrived in Sochi, but then his fever caused him to sleep around the clock for two days.

The last night in Tbilisi we were taken to a restaurant for a real Georgian dinner. It was the same food we had been given at every meal on the trip except that the Georgians like everything peppery hot. We were crowded into two rooms at the restaurant, seated at long tables and entertained by costumed singers and instrumentalists. My father would have said, "Well, they can't sing good, but they can sing loud!" Conversation took place at a screaming level to rise above the din of the "music." Wine flowed freely and everyone had a good time.

Another evening we were escorted to an old, partially ruined church and were truly entertained by marvelous Georgian dancers. The stark ruins of stone walls made a perfect setting for the dancers and created an atmosphere of austerity and mysticism. We found ourselves journeying back in history as we watched the flamboyant displays of technique. The men in soft shoes danced on their toes like ballerinas. They leapt to amazing heights and landed on the tips of their toes. It was a fantastic evening of music, brilliantly costumed dancers, whirling swords and spine-tingling harmonies.

Sam was having difficulty walking on the cobbled streets and climbing the hills and staircases to reach places of interest. It was strenuous walking for everyone, but Sam's arthritic hip pained him, and the leg which had undergone three by-passes tired easily and became numb. He either sat in the bus during the stops or elected not to take the tour at all, resting in the hotel in relative comfort.

There was some question whether we would be allowed to go to Yerevan, the capital of Armenia. Demonstrations were being held, primarily on weekends, and we were scheduled to arrive on a Saturday. The demonstrations had not been violent, but the situation was becoming more critical every day. It was finally decided that we could proceed. We boarded the bus for a full day's drive. All along the route, called Friendship Highway since it links Georgia with Armenia, the views were lovely. Mount Ararat seen from Yerevan is a moving sight, towering to the sky across the border in Turkey. I tried to imagine my brother, Bill, climbing and exploring the heights of such an imposing mysterious monument. Climb it he did in 1983, but at the edge of victory, when they believed that only a few more feet of digging would expose the Ark, a blinding blizzard drove the party off the mountain. Throughout the ages, men have attempted the treacherous ascent in search of the Ark, but it remains elusive.

One stop we made enroute would remain in all our minds. It was the "pit stop" by the side of the road. It was literally the pits. The men refused to enter the filthy stall and took to the bushes instead. It was worse than any outhouse, dark, putrid holes dug in the floor and obviously never attended to. The odor clung all about the area. Unfortunately, this was the type of toilet found in all public places in the Soviet Union. On the ground floor of one hotel the "rest rooms" were positioned right outside the dining room. To get to and from we had to hold our breaths against the odor. Sanitation seemed to be nonexistent.

By contrast, one could have eaten off the streets, they were so clean. "Grandmothers" with head scarves tied under their chins could be seen everywhere, industriously sweeping up little piles of leaves and papers from the sidewalks and streets. Not a scrap remained after the great dump trucks had rumbled along, scooping up the dainty piles at every block. Yet the public toilets were disgusting, ill used and seemed never to be cleaned.

❦

The weekend in Yerevan was interesting. Our hotel was slightly better than the one in Tbilisi, though still run-down. It was situated on Lenin Square, a vast area surrounded by shops and offices, with a monument of "The Hero" dominating center stage.

Judy and Ann, still in the throes of bronchitis, elected to skip the day tour to wander about the square. They had an adventure which they considered the highlight of the trip. An elderly, attractive woman approached them with smiles to ask, in broken English, if they were British. When Judy said, "No, Americans," she became elated and clapped her hands, exclaiming, "Reagan, Reagan Reagan!" to show her delight with America. She then walked along with the girls, recounting her life story.

She was a piano teacher, a graduate of Leningrad Conservatory, and had always lived in Yerevan. When Ann told her that their mother was also a piano teacher and about the same age, the lady's warmth became even more marked. She insisted on buying them a gift of candy and told them to choose whatever they liked. They made an unfortunate choice. The candy proved inedible and the lady had purchased a kilo of it.

Judy and Ann loved the day with their new friend and took her picture, which they later mailed to her. The woman confided that she had been saving her money for years in order to make a trip to the States. Now, we wonder what has become of her since the disastrous earthquake which occurred just one month after we returned home.

On Saturday, as we returned from our tour, we passed a huge crowd of young people gathered for another demonstration in the square. Banners and posters held high, they were smiling and friendly, having a good time together. There was nothing ominous about the crowd. They waved to us in the bus. We smiled and returned the greetings.

Our room did not look out over the Square, but others in our group reported a great deal of activity which lasted most of the night. It became noisier by the hour, but it was more a festive gathering than one intent on promoting violence. The ascending volume of shouting was evidently induced by too much vodka.

We were roused at 4:30 a.m. on Sunday morning to depart for the airport. Our plane for Sochi was to leave at 7:30. We had a fair breakfast in the dining room at the airport, but could not face the intolerable restroom before boarding for the flight to Sochi, the principal beach resort in the Soviet Union. This is the only tropical area in that vast country, attractive with beautiful gardens. The boulevards are lined with tropical plants and flowers, and the beach on the Black Sea is extensive with many hotels lining the shore. It reminded us of Miami Beach.

The weather had been wonderfully warm throughout our trip, and we were told Sochi would be the warmest of all. Everyone brought bathing suits and looked forward to swimming and relaxing on the beach, as this was the only chance for our group to rest and prepare for the final two days in Moscow before returning home. Unfortunately, we blew into Sochi on the heels of a cyclone. It was cold and windy, uncomfortable and bleak. We only saw the beach from the hotel window, a deserted black stretch of rocks with little sand. A few brave souls tried the swimming pool.

Sam had a full-fledged cold by now. He went to bed feeling miserable and slept away the two days we were there. I brought him tea and apples from the dining room, but he was too sick to want them. After seeing the doctor, he began antibiotics. Judy and Ann were still coughing and were anxious for the tour to end. Though many in our group were ill, the virus had not caught up with me.

We spent a long afternoon at a tea plantation high in the hills beyond Sochi. It was a gorgeous day, cool and sunny, and the views were splendid. The hillsides were covered with rows of tea bushes, carefully tended by teams of workers. An elderly man gave us a long, detailed explanation about the history and cultivation of tea, made longer by the need for translation by the guide. We sat in rows on wooden benches under the pine trees, half-listening, but more absorbed with the view across the richly green, undulating land.

After the oration, we walked down the road to a log house, where we were served a typical Russian tea. Bowls of the ever-present apples and bowls of nuts, which we cracked ourselves, sat on the tables, as well as plates of pretty cakes. The tea was delicious, poured from a samovar at the end of each table by attractive girls in Russian peasant dresses with ribbons in their hair. A group of musicians played enchanting folk music on balalaikas. The atmosphere of Old Russia, as I had understood it from story books, came alive.

It was the most pleasant afternoon of entertainment on the tour. Back at the hotel, I was distressed to find Sam still in bed, flushed with fever and weak. He told me he had been experiencing more chest pain than usual. I suggested that perhaps the antibiotics might be conflicting with his other medications. He had many pills to take every day. Though we had been told the chest pains were not due to a heart problem, it was disquieting to have "spasms of the lower esophagus" last so many months. He agreed that the antibiotics might be making him worse and stopped taking them before he had quite finished the series.

The next morning he felt much better. The chest pains had stopped. He had a good breakfast, and we boarded our last Aeroflot plane for the flight to Moscow.

It was a distance of one thousand miles and took a long seven hours, but we arrived safely at 5:30 p.m. and were driven to the Cosmos Hotel. There was a farewell party before dinner with gifts to our two special Marinas, who were by now much beloved companions. They had been of great help to everyone.

The Cosmos Hotel was a relief after all the poor accommodations for the past week. It was up-to-date and had a contemporary decor. Still, it was a rabbit warren of tourists. We were amazed to see dozens of Intourist buses lined up for tours. They were in and out every hour day and night. We were told that Moscow was a city of nine million people plus two million tourists. It was a crowded, busy, bustling place with row after row of concrete buildings on every street. Someone asked what one word might describe the country. "Uniformity" was my immediate response. The food was nearly the same every place we went. We ate on the same white, gold-rimmed china and matching glassware. We wiped off crumbs with an occasional paper napkin the size of one square of toilet paper. The bread, either white or tan, tasted as if it had all come from the same bakery. Apples were plentiful, apple juice for breakfast and bowls of apples on the table for dessert. The poured concrete buildings presented a uniform appearance, and the bureaucracy followed rules steadfastly with no deviation.

The last day in Moscow, we were taken to the Kremlin and admitted to the Armory, which, I gathered, was a special treat. Again Sam forfeited the tour. He was increasingly in pain when he walked. He would also grow short of breath and then a chest pain would begin. His hip hurt and his leg was numb. Even a short walk seemed too much. He decided to rest during the day because he wanted to enjoy our final evening at the Moscow Circus. We were all looking forward to that special event.

The Armory housed a fabulous display of treasures, gifts presented to the long line of Tsars throughout the ages. Cabinets were stuffed with gold objects—statuary, vases and bowls, jewelry encrusted with rare gems, all manner of beautiful and extravagant ware. One huge cabinet contained silver of all kinds—priceless urns, hollowware, mirrors and art objects. There were coronation robes of gold cloth trimmed with ermine, crowns, gowns of the Tsarinas with their fans and furs, taxidermed horses saddled and bridled in gold and silver set with gems. It was the most splendid array of costly artifacts imaginable.

I could not have believed such a gaudy collection of treasures could be assembled in one place. Restoration was such that each item was in perfect condition. It was mind-boggling to realize that only one-fourth of the Imperial collection remained. The rest had been destroyed, carried off or lost during the Revolution. What was left had been preserved with great care, seemingly a priority of the government and a tremendous tourist attraction.

My general impression of Russia was that anything that would be viewed by a visitor was in excellent order. The appearance of the cities was neat, very clean and up-to-date. But we learned from the guides and from our own experience that those who ventured within the freshly painted buildings found an opposite situation. Families are crowded into two room apartments; sanitation is deplorable; food is scarce; people are unable to buy nice clothes or practical appliances and furniture for their homes. The amenities we take for granted are almost non-existent. The famous Gum Department Store, an immense building, has only strange, rag-like clothes hanging from the racks. People stand in line for everything. Restaurants provide poor service and, usually, poorer food. The inner workings of the country are in need of much repair, yet the gold of the statues and domes of the buildings shine with brilliance and splendor.

We had quite a long drive to the great, round contemporary building which is the home of the Moscow Circus. It is one of the best shows of its kind that any of us had ever seen, with one ring only. The marvelous acrobats, high wire artists, fantastically trained animals—birds, dogs, horses, seals, bears and monkeys—performed acts to astound and excite. We enjoyed every minute of it.

As we left the building after the show, rain was pouring down as it had been ever since we arrived in Moscow, but the buses were parked not too far away. Sam suddenly stopped with another pain. "Take the umbrella and go on to the bus," he told me, "I'll be right along.

He needed a free hand to reach for his nitrostat. I went on as he instructed me, found a seat for us near the rear of the bus, and Sam followed a moment later. He pulled himself through the door and up the steps, and my heart sank to see him look so gray. It seemed to take a great effort for him to walk to our seat. He moved slowly, his head bent from the strain. As he sat down, he closed his eyes and said, "I'm in real trouble. I'll have to see the doctor as soon as we get home." I replied that I thought we should have a wheelchair ready for him at the airport. He answered, "I think it would be a goo---" His voice trailed off and I looked up quickly to see why he hadn't finished his sentence.

His face was contorted into a terrible grimace, his lips drawn back over his teeth. Death was in his face. In shock, I watched him struggle for breath. I grabbed his arm and called his name over and over, but he was in spasms of torture. Terrible shuddering sounds came from his throat and his body stiffened in agony. After three or more violent shudders, I felt him go completely limp and fall back in his seat. I knew the moment his heart stopped and told myself, "It's all over. He's gone."

I was unable to speak or move. Someone back of us called out, "Stop the bus. We're having trouble back here." Two men rushed back to see what they could do for Sam. They were the only doctors in our group and both happened to be on our bus. They picked him up somehow and carried him to the back of the bus where there was a long bench and began CPR, trying to revive his heart. The wife of one of the doctors was a nurse. She timed the efforts of the doctors, who took turns working on his chest with all their strength. After eight minutes Sam's heart responded, but still the doctors continued with their hard rhythmic pressing on his chest and breathing down his throat.

The bus drove to a nearby hospital, having commandeered a passing car to lead us there. We sat waiting at the emergency entrance with a crew of nurses. They waited in the pelting rain until the doctors thought it was safe to move Sam from the bus to a stretcher. Judy and Ann had left their seats at the forward end of the bus to come sit with me. We held each other for comfort, unable to do more than pray. Dead silence hung over the bus.

Finally Sam was carried to the stretcher by the doctors and several nurses. We followed him into the hospital along with Philip Ryan and Marina One. As Sam was wheeled into the emergency room, I was horrified to see his bare feet a cyanotic blue. Circulation had ceased in his legs. They had removed his clothes in the bus and covered him with blankets.

Judy, Ann and I found a wooden bench in the dingy, dark hallway and sat waiting for an endless hour. Judy left to explore the passageway. When she returned she told me, "Mother, whatever you do, don't go to the bathroom. It is unspeakable." Soon, Ann decided she couldn't wait any longer and went down the hall. When she returned she said, "Mother, whatever you do, don't go there." I thought, "What does it matter?" I started down the hall. Just then the doctors Snow and Frankel came out with Philip and Marina.

They assured us it would be all right to leave. Sam had been put in a respirator and was receiving intravenous medication. As it was one o'clock in the morning and taxis had been ordered for us, we left Sam in the emergency room and went back to the hotel. I felt lost and bewildered by the terrible turn of events. What would we be able to do from now on? Would Sam survive? I was numb with shock and unable to think clearly beyond the urgent need to call home and alert someone who could notify everyone that we would not be home the next day. I called Dottie Ritter, who I knew would be home at that time and able to relay messages to those who were expecting us.

The next dreary day began when we met at breakfast. Philip and Marina stayed by our side, and we taxied back to the hospital, where Sam was still unconscious. I took all of Sam's medicines to show the doctor and, with Marina to translate, explained Sam's general condition and medical history. The doctor was concerned about Sam's lungs. With congestive heart failure, fluid builds up in the lungs and there is danger of pneumonia.

Depressed and worried, we left the hospital for the U.S. Embassy. Philip had made an appointment with the Vice-Consul, Stephen Walker. We arrived at the Embassy and were astounded by the crowd on the street waiting for an entry. The waiting room was overflowing with people wanting travel visas or needing to discuss other problems. They were not Americans and looked askance at us as we filed past them, our group of five gaining access to the office without a moment's delay.

We found Vice-Consul Walker and his secretary very pleasant and concerned. They offered help and made themselves available for anything within their power. However, it was too soon to know what might develop at the hospital and too soon to move Sam to a better facility if there was one.

We were distressed to find the hospital such a pitiful place, antiquated, run-down and none too clean. Sam was in an intensive care unit that also seemed to serve as the recovery room for surgical patients. It was bare and reminded us of scenes from the World War I movie, *Farewell to Arms*. The equipment was old. Sam was laid on a stretcher-bed, covered with a sheet. He looked so cold. I had brought his favorite slippers as well as his comb, toothbrush and razor, but one look at the terrible tube thrust down his throat told me he would have no use for anything but slippers on his cold, blue feet. I asked if I might put them on. I knew he wouldn't be comfortable without them, as he had always worn them, even in bed, ever since his last by-pass nine months before.

The team of doctors were eager to help and smiled their understanding and compassion, but verbal communication was nearly impossible. Only one doctor had any understanding of English, and his was very limited. I understood they needed my permission to give Sam a blood transfusion. They hoped this would create better circulation and permit him to breathe on his own without the respirator.

Sam was conscious when we returned later that morning. His eyes filled with tears of distress when he saw me. His expression conveyed such a look of apology that he had caused any problem for me that I fought to keep back the tears. He tried to speak, but, of course, could not. I said, "Please don't try to talk and please don't worry. We are all right. We're going to get home as soon as possible." I tried to reassure him and keep my voice calm, but I was so sick inside I couldn't look into his eyes. I busied myself with a pen and a pad of paper and showed him I wanted him to write.

There were two questions I had to ask. "Do we have travel insurance?" Sam shook his head. Then, "How much credit is on our Mastercard?" He held up five fingers. "Five thousand dollars?" He nodded.

My heart sank, but I could not let him know how frightened I was. He needed strength and courage from me, not panic. I asked him to write down any questions or anything he might need. He was stripped of all his clothes. I had taken them away the night before when Philip handed me the bundle with his watch and wallet.

Sam took the pen and struggled to write. His handwriting was tiny and strange, barely legible. "I don't remember how I got here," he scribbled. I told him he had had a heart attack, that Dr. Snow and Dr. Frankel were on the bus with us and had saved his life. I asked him to rest and get well. Sam frowned and struggled again with the pen.

"What surgery?" He was worried, thinking of another operation. Obviously, the doctor had tried to get his permission for the transfusion.

"Oh, no surgery, Sam. The doctor just wants to give you a blood transfusion. I tried to keep my voice light and smiled at the young doctor on the other side of the stretcher-table.

"A transfusion with Aids, Doctor?" I joked. The doctor stiffened and looked me straight in the eye.

"No Aids, Russia!" he said. Then we both smiled. Sam relaxed and closed his eyes. I tiptoed out.

We sat with our group at lunch. It was all we could do to swallow the food past the big lumps in our throats. Our new-found friends pressed rubles into our hands along with packages of Kleenex, books to read, life savers, gum and odds and ends they would not need—because *they* were going home. One couple handed me a roll of dollars. When I protested, they told me to take the money and mail it back to them later if I wished, but they intended it as a gift. Later, when I opened the roll and counted it, I was overwhelmed. They had given me five hundred dollars! Someone else handed me one hundred, another twenty-five. Philip Ryan had bought two hundred rubles for me on the black market, and more fell into our hands from the sudden friendships forged in just a few hours.

After pooling our funds, I put the five hundred dollars in a separate compartment in my purse, determined not to spend it unless I had to. We were short of cash and had cashed in all our rubles the day before in anticipation of returning home. The gifts of rubles were most welcome. Sam had five hundred dollars in his wallet, and I had less than two hundred plus twelve hundred dollars in travelers checks. Sam's checks were useless to me, but I had him sign one of his personal checks that morning in the hospital. I planned to fill it out later for five thousand in order to repay Mastercard for charges we would incur in air fare and hotel bills. Judy and Ann would have to fly home in a few days, then the check could be mailed, and I would have a fresh five thousand on which to draw.

My frightening thought was the length of time we might have to remain in Moscow. The doctors had indicated it would be at least three or four weeks before Sam could be moved, provided he could be taken off the respirator.

The thought of Judy and Ann leaving me alone filled me with panic, but I couldn't ask them to stay. They had obligations at home. Ann had a new business, a shop in Boulder. Christmas merchandise had to be ordered. Judy had planned to move back to Indianapolis from the Cape and her dog had been languishing in a kennel overlong, costing big bucks every day. I felt they should look after their own affairs, but still could hardly bear the thought of their leaving. I had to think of the cost. If they stayed with me, it would be multiplied by three. They had limited funds which could not cover the bills we would be facing.

After lunch, the Alumni Holiday group assembled in one of the public rooms for the last lecture. Judy, Ann and I waited in an anteroom, disconsolate and silent with our own brooding thoughts of the tragedy. We wanted to see everyone off and be with them as long as we could. We would miss their support. At four o'clock they gathered in the Cosmos lobby, and with despair we watched them leave. At that moment we became abandoned tourists. The hundreds of other milling strangers in the lobby were not concerned with us. We returned to our rooms, knowing that at least dear Marina One would be back to join us for dinner after she had seen her charges safely through airport customs.

The phone rang, jangling my nerves. A voice was speaking in broken English. I realized it was the friendly doctor trying to communicate. "Your husband—small better," he managed to say. I thanked him for his thoughtfulness and let him know I would be there in the morning. In spite of the difficulties of dealing with foreign people in a foreign land, I felt and appreciated the helpful kindness of strangers, even though there was little anyone could do in such a crisis.

Marina returned at 6:00 p.m. and stayed with us until her train left for Leningrad at 9:30. She took us to a different restaurant in the hotel. Now that we were separated from our group, we could no longer eat in the usual dining room. We ate in a cafeteria where we paid a fixed price before entering, then had the choice of a large buffet—as much of it as we liked. Unfortunately, the food was all too familiar. We had no appetite and only ate to keep up our strength for the days to come. The main course was heavy and greasy, but the soup was rich and filling. We survived on soup, bread and fruit.

Marina spent the entire time during dinner writing instructions for us in both English and Russian. To hire a taxi, it was necessary to order it the night before and show the hospital's address to both the desk clerk and the taxi driver; we could not expect to pick up a taxi on the street; it would take a taxi at least two hours to respond after being called. Marina added a note to the driver pleading him to wait for us, which they were usually unwilling to do. All of them did wait, but the drive to and from the hospital took forty-five minutes and the fare was expensive. Most of our rubles were used for taxis, as every other place only accepted dollars.

Marina gave us great comfort as long as she was with us. She told us our visas would be extended by the Intourist Bureau and our hotel rooms would be ours for as long as we needed them, with only a slight increase in rate. She gave us directions about using the Metro and suggested some possible activities for us. She assured us the Intourist Bureau would look after us, help with our air fares when we were ready to leave and escort us to the airport. They would also be on hand to help with translations or provide guides if we needed them.

Marina believed what she told us and thought she had taken care of us. She had even bribed Intourist with gifts she had received as tips when our group left. Guides were not permitted to accept money, but cigarettes, candy, items of clothing and music tapes were allowable gifts to the guides in appreciation of their services. In spite of Marina's bribes, we were given the cold shoulder by everyone connected to Intourist. We had to go it alone with the occasional help of a passing stranger. Ordinary people came to our aid, as well as the U.S. Embassy, but we got no help from the bureaucrats sitting with authority behind their desks. They were intractable.

After Marina left us, we retired to our rooms and tried to sleep. We had ordered a taxi, per instructions, for the next morning. We encountered no difficulty. Promptly on the half hour we watched for the license number of the cab and, when it appeared, we took our first ride to the hospital without an escort.

Entering the hospital, we passed through the ill-lighted hallway and up a flight of stairs to reach a sort of office, where doctors convened during rest periods. Two desks, a dilapidated sofa and two straight chairs filled the room completely. On one wall were shelves containing an electric coffee maker, odds and ends of dishes, the remains of half-eaten buns and cups of leftover coffee. The pile of unwashed dishes shocked us because we expected a hospital to be a sanitary place. Dust lay on the furniture. The doctors wore wrinkled, unwashed coats that once were white, with matching caps on their heads. The coats and caps were obviously exchangeable from one to another because we were given coats from the rack to wear when entering intensive care. I was not pleased to put one on, worn before, who knows how many times. Still, I complied and waited to be led down the corridor to the ward. The three of us took turns going in—not because anybody indicated that we should, but because we knew that in the hospitals at home only one person at a time would be allowed to enter an intensive care unit.

I was encouraged to see Sam slightly propped up on the stretcher. I didn't stay long as I didn't want to tire him. I assured him that we were working on a way to get us all home soon. After a brief visit, I left so that Judy and Ann could take their turns.

I was worried about Ann, who was still coughing. Because of her tendency to lung inflammation and pneumonia, I asked the doctor to give her medicine and to X-ray her chest. She disappeared for a long time. Concerned that we might lose the waiting taxi, I left the hospital and sat with the driver in his cab. The girls finally came out after Judy had also had an X-ray. Ann did have pneumonia, which the doctor said was on the wane, and Judy had bronchitis. About this time I felt the beginnings of a sore throat. We all began a series of antibiotics.

The weather didn't help our illnesses. Rain was incessant. A cold, ominous wind heralded winter. Our flimsy clothes were inadequate. We were sick and suffering from worry. After we returned to the hotel, things went from bad to worse. I checked with the office to be sure our rooms would not be usurped by incoming tourists. The manager was concerned when I told her we might be there for some time. She wanted to know how we planned to pay, "It is very expensive here," she said.

"How expensive?" I asked.

"The rooms are ninety rubles a day, forty more than you paid with the tour group now that you are no longer with them."

I remonstrated that our guide had told us the rate increase would not exceed ten rubles a day. The manager stood firm. She offered to put us all in one room, but I felt the coughing that went on in the girls' room would rob me of necessary rest. I told her we would manage somehow. She offered to put me up in a less expensive hotel, but I was afraid of transferring to a place without a recommendation. I told her we would stay through the weekend and then make a decision.

In the meantime, the girls had checked to see if our visas had been extended as promised. Nothing had been done. We were in the country illegally. It was another day before our visas were in order. The hotel, of course, was still holding our passports.

Judy and Ann were anxious to return home. We decided to go to the Lufthansa office to see whether we could get credit on our return air fares. We were lucky enough to find a taxi, but the driver had no idea where Lufthansa was. We drove around and around. Finally, Judy decided to try to phone them when she spotted a phone booth on the street. While standing in line to use the phone, she struck up a conversation with a girl who understood a little English. The girl said she knew where the office was and we could walk there.

We paid off the cab and followed the girl, who left her boy friend standing on the curb while she escorted us to the office which turned out to be Italia instead of Lufthansa. Apologizing profusely for her mistake, she left us, and we entered to get directions from the English speaking clerk.

We found the Lufthansa office only a block away, but had to wait an hour for the manager to return from lunch. He finally showed up at three o'clock for our two o'clock appointment. He was pleasant enough and made reservations for the girls for the following Wednesday, but he laughed when we asked him for some credit on the return fare.

"You already had credit. You came over with your group on half fare. The credit is used up."

I wanted to pay for their tickets with my Mastercard, but he said he couldn't accept money for the tickets: "All air fares must be paid for in an Aeroflot office. We can only make reservations."

The bureaucratic run-around wore us out with frustration. Now we needed a taxi, and the Lufthansa manager did not explain how we could make one stop for us. All the empty cabs sailed by. After a desperate half hour of walking and flagging, we jumped into a cab momentarily stopped for a light, and the driver had no choice but to take us back to the Cosmos, where we learned the only Aeroflot office that would accept money for our fares was in the Hotel Continental. We had had it for the day.

I had seen a notice at the tour desk (Intourist, of course) that the Bolshoi Ballet would be performing that weekend. I thought I would get tickets and provide a little entertainment for the girls. I asked the woman at the desk for three tickets, but I was told I couldn't buy them. I must return in the morning when she would have plenty of seats available.

Back in my lonely room after some food in the cafeteria, I was startled to hear the phone ringing. It was the first of three calls.

The doctor reported on Sam's condition, again saying he was "small better." At the next ring, I was surprised and grateful to hear Marina's voice calling from Leningrad to inquire about Sam and how we were faring. I nearly burst into tears. I told her about the lack of attention and coöperation from Intourist. She was not too surprised. Later, I wrote two letters: one to Marina full of our deepest thanks for her help and concern, the other to her superior at the Leningrad office. I hoped she would be rewarded by the praise in my letter, and I also wanted her boss to know about the lack of cooperation of everyone else connected with the Bureau. Marina had given us service well beyond her duties as a guide, and I wanted her superiors to know how superior she was. Hopefully, she might be given a raise.

The last call of the night was a great surprise and gave me a new feeling of security in this alien land. The young, lilting voice introduced herself as Tanya Hudson, a friend of one of the doctors caring for Sam. She offered to translate or give any other help we required. She told me to call her at work or at home as her parents both spoke English and could take messages for her. I almost wept with relief. I knew I would call her if only to thank her for stretching out her hand to us. I was also touched by the doctors' concern and their having the foresight to alert someone who could speak for us and come to our aid if needed.

I slept more easily that night knowing help was around the corner.

Saturday morning I was first in line when the Intourist theater desk opened. I was told I would have to return later in the day to see if tickets were available. I reminded the clerk that she had promised there would be plenty of seats, but to no avail. "Very sorry. Next please!" She waved me away. When I returned later, I was told to come back tomorrow. I decided to move to another hotel. I called the Embassy. They suggested the Belgrade Hotel. It was near the Embassy, only half as far from the hospital and less expensive.

We were able to reserve two rooms beginning on Sunday. The rates were sixty rubles for my single room and seventy for the girls' double. We would have a better rate than at the Cosmos, as well as a location closer to the hospital.

Saturday afternoon the girls tried again to get airline tickets for the States. We taxied to the Continental Hotel, which amazed us by its splendor. It was elegant, contemporary and enormous, a match for the finest hotel anywhere. We rose on escalators to the high reaches of the mezzanine, where glamorous stores displayed their wares. A beriozka shop had priceless treasures for sale, such as we had not seen in any part of Russia. There were dress shops with stunning clothes for men and women—rich mink and sable coats and priceless jewelry. We could not believe our eyes.

At the Aeroflot office we were again denied the opportunity to pay for the air reservations. It was Saturday. "Come back Monday," they told us.

We spent a little time browsing in the shops, which included a superb grocery, selling only gourmet imported items and accepting only dollars for the merchandise. We learned later that the Continental was built with Armand Hammer money, Mr. Hammer being a great benefactor of Russia. His home in Moscow is open for tourists, and he himself is highly honored by the government. His wife was Russian. He fell in love, not only with her, but with the country and its people. Of all the aristocratic homes in Moscow, his alone was not touched during the Revolution.

We had no trouble finding a taxi at the Continental. Several were waiting at the entrance. This was not a tourist establishment. No Intourist bus was in sight. The vast lobby and mezzanine were all but deserted. We couldn't help but wonder who frequented this hotel—probably the wealthiest of foreigners.

At the reservation desk in the Cosmos, we were told we could not buy tickets for the ballet because we were not in a tour group. Intourist simply could not be bothered with incidental people like us. My back was up and I decided to pursue the purchase of tickets at the Belgrade, but at that hotel also there was a negative response. Judy persevered, insisting on service, and we were finally rewarded with three tickets.

The only hitch was that the ballet would be performed in the Kremlin Auditorium, as the Bolshoi Theater was closed for repairs. We would have to get there by Metro. Frightened of the unknown subway and walking at night in the cold and rain, I would have given up at that point, but the girls persuaded me to give it a try. They promised to find the way for us and indeed they did. We plodded through deep puddles for several blocks, only making a couple of wrong turns. Once inside the Metro, we again found support from helpful strangers who happily showed us the way. We arrived at the theater intact and not too wet. To my delight, our seats in the beautiful auditorium (all red, of course) were excellent. We were seated with a group of English tourists.

The ballet transported us out of gloom and despair and brought us a little hope. *Les Sylphides* put us in a trance, but the highlight of the evening was a *Pas de Deux* danced so magically that at its conclusion the audience went mad. They yelled, stamped and clapped in unison. Many bouquets were showered on the principals. A good half of the audience raced down to the footlights, applauding and cheering. We were amazed by the riotous reception. The English tourists informed us that the ballerina was considered a national treasure and was sixty-three years old. She seemed so young and danced with the grace and flexibility of a girl in her twenties. The *Pas de Deux* was "The Withering Rose" with music by Mahler.

The evening gave us just what we needed to break from the pall of anxiety under which we were suffering, but because of our efforts to buy air flights that morning and the move to the Belgrade in the afternoon, we had had to miss our trip to the hospital.

The Hotel Belgrade was a come-down from the Cosmos. The lobby was a seething mass of "secondary" tourists. At least my tiny room was cozy and clean. I even had a television set that worked once in a while. The Summer Olympics were on in Seoul, Korea and the programs beamed over by satellite showed a predominance of Russian athletes. They were marvelous and were taking all the medals. I watched as much as I could, staying in my room to be close to the phone. The girls objected to their room because it was full of stale tobacco smoke. They gagged and choked even after they aired the place out, opening windows to the freezing elements. They said they coughed all night, but by the next day the odor was gone.

The hotel restaurant was better than the ones we had become used to. It had a different menu, though we couldn't read it, and the food was more appetizing. It was a coöperative, owned and managed by a group of citizens rather than the government. Service was faster and more civil; prices were lower, and the huge room was reasonably attractive. We always went in early to escape the massive tour groups.

Sunday morning when we taxied to the hospital, we were dismayed to learn that Sam had undergone a very bad day on Saturday. He lay exhausted, not wishing to be roused, but he did know we were there. His kidneys had failed and dialysis had been performed. His kidneys were functioning again, but it had been hard on him. It was a terrible setback. Hope of his recovery had diminished. The doctors were unable to explain that he also had pneumonia. They managed to convey the information that they wanted to give him two more days to improve, after which it wouldn't make much difference if he was moved to another facility or even out of the country.

The Lufthansa doctor who had examined Sam reported to us that there was no possibility of transporting him to the States on a commercial airliner since the respirator could not be removed. He implied that Sam's condition was hopeless.

I called the U.S. Embassy and Vice-Consul Walker advised that if we wished to move Sam on an air ambulance, we could call upon Europ Assistance, an organization in Washington D.C. He wished to see Sam and came that very day, picking us up on the way. When he did see Sam, he was shocked and particularly disturbed by the condition of the hospital. He agreed that it was imperative to get him to Paris, where he could receive the best possible treatment in a clean, modern facility.

I called Washington as soon as we returned to the hotel and was relieved to hear a confident, reassuring voice at the other end asking pertinent questions about our finances. I told Jeff Kirkman the state of credit on my Mastercard and the condition Sam was in. He took the number of the credit card, said he would contact their representative doctor in Moscow and request that she see Sam to determine what would be necessary for transportation. Twenty minutes later, he called back to report that he had telephoned our bank and requested unlimited credit due to the emergency situation. Frank Springer and Nick Kaiser had been asked to vouch for our credit and it was granted by the bank. Unknown to us, Sam's sister Polly had been calling Frank and Nick from Florida asking for help. She and Don were ready to leave for England and planned to come to our aid from there.

Knowing we had unlimited credit made all the difference. We couldn't move a step without funds. When told that the cost of the air ambulance would be $22,000, I was stunned, but still glad that I could pay it. We had to get Sam and ourselves out of Russia.

After that first call, Jeff became our hero. Things moved swiftly. He took care of everything, reserving air flights, hotel rooms in Paris and ambulance service from the American Hospital. Sam would be on a plane in two days.

In the meantime, Judy and Ann stopped trying to leave Moscow and decided to wait until we could all leave together. Not having been able to pay for their reservations had been a lucky stroke after all. Providence stepped in to keep us together.

I called Tanya Hudson to thank her for her generosity and to invite her and her husband to dinner so we could meet and repay her somewhat for her kindness to us. I spoke to her mother and father. They were both friendly and warm. Tanya explained that her husband was in Annapolis, Maryland, studying law. She planned to leave for the States in two months to join him and live there permanently. I was surprised that her husband, Brian Hudson, was American and that she would be given permission to leave the Soviet Union. They had met when he was a student in Moscow and had married just three months later. I could hardly wait to meet her. I told her we might have a connection with her husband as I was a descendant of Heinrich Hudson through my Grandmother Ball.

Tanya came to the hotel on Tuesday night, our last night in Moscow. She arrived at my room straight from work and took time to comb her windblown hair and hang her damp coat up to dry. As usual, the weather was miserable, but she was obviously used to it. She was lovely. Long, dark hair and matching eyelashes over large brown eyes set off her pretty face. She was also vivacious, and it was no wonder she had found a young man who was head-over-heels in love with her.

We went to a dining room a floor above our usual one. It was a smaller, more intimate room with white tablecloths. Only a few tables were occupied. We were shown to our table by a young, willowy waiter who smiled, bowed and flourished his hands extravagantly. He reminded me of the late movie comedian, Mischa Auer.

At last we had an interpreter and could order more than borscht. Tanya explained the menu, describing how the dishes were prepared. After he had taken our order, the waiter sailed away, obviously delighted to serve three beautiful girls, one of whom he could converse with. Soon he returned and, with flourishes extraordinaire, produced a bottle of champagne, uncorking it before we could protest that it had not been ordered. Tanya understood that the champagne was a gift from the gentlemen sitting directly behind us. I turned around in astonishment, smiled an acknowledgement and thought—now what are we in for? We drank a toast to them as we sipped our champagne while waiting for dinner to arrive.

Tanya announced she couldn't drink because she was pregnant. We were excited to hear her news and fell into discussion about her trip to Maryland. She was sorrowful about leaving her parents. She felt she would have to become a U.S. citizen before undertaking future visits to Russia, and she hated to think of living away from her family for the five years it would take to establish citizenship. Judy did not want much champagne and Ann none at all, so the lion's share fell to me. I needed the lift badly.

We enjoyed our dinner and the fellowship. I was relieved when the men took their leave without saying another word—just nodding as they left. They had merely been friendly and hospitable. But, during the meal, we had noticed our waiter becoming increasingly gallant, bowing and scraping and giving us much attention. We felt he was enjoying pick-me-ups in the recesses of the kitchen. At dessert time, he flashed a bottle of wine in front of me and, with a Mischa Auer bow, indicated it was a gift from himself! I begged Tanya to thank him, but as I had polished off most of the champagne I left him to enjoy most of the wine he had intended for us.

The dinner was the highlight of a dreary week. Our spirits were lifted by the charming, lovely Tanya. After a short visit in my room, she left us to return home in the rain via Metro. I was concerned for her alone on the streets at night, but she assured me there was nothing to fear in Russia where crimes of violence are practically unknown.

Wednesday was a blur of packing, checking out of the hotel (not without difficulty) and then waiting many hours at the airport. Judy and Ann went to the hospital with a "care package" of thanks for the doctors' compassionate, competent care. We knew there would be no bill to pay at the hospital and could think of no other way to show our gratitude. The doctors had done everything possible for Sam in spite of inferior hospital conditions. Specialists from around the city had been called in to examine Sam.

They had prescribed drugs to keep him comfortable on his miserable stretcher. He received four transfusions and kidney dialysis as well as being monitored by the respirator and heart machine.

We bought a bottle of Amaretto liquor for $43, a carton of Marlboros for $20 (Russians prize American cigarettes), and some candy. We also included most of a very large bottle of vodka which Sam had purchased in Frankfort. I stayed in my room to receive important phone calls with instructions from Jeff Kirkman. The girls returned from the hospital reporting that the doctors were not very receptive to our gifts. We had thought they would appreciate a token of thanks, but later wondered if they feared to accept anything for fear of being accused of accepting bribes. At any rate, Judy and Ann left the package and departed without seeing Sam, as he was being prepared for transportation to Paris. We had told him the day before that we were all going to Paris. He showed surprise and puzzlement, but fell asleep before we could explain.

The doctor from Europ Assistance came to the hotel to help us check out. I was fortunate she was with me to translate as the cashier spoke no English and did not want to accept rubles to pay any part of the bill. She finally agreed when the doctor interceded. I needed to spend all the rubles before leaving the country as rubles were not allowed out of the U.S.S.R.

The doctor was frantic to get back to the hospital where she had much to do for Sam's departure. Papers needed to be signed and Sam had to be seen safely aboard the air ambulance. She hurried off, explaining that her husband would drive us to the airport.

Our bags were in the lobby, and we were ready when Aram appeared. He was charming and spoke much better English than his doctor wife. He told us he was a math professor at the University of Moscow who had been commandeered by his wife for this errand. He had been glad to oblige and stuck it out with us hour after hour at the airport.

As usual, there was trouble over buying our tickets through to Paris. Europ Assistance had reserved space for us on British Airways to London, then on to Paris as there was no through flight that day. This proved to be a lucky break because the ticket seller refused to accept more than $1000 on a credit card, and each ticket to Paris cost $1400. After much discussion and interpretation by Aram, she finally agreed to sell us tickets only as far as London. We could pay the additional fare on arrival. She demanded three credit cards. This was a problem as Ann's credit was used up and Judy had only $700 left on hers and I had my Mastercard. In a flash, I remembered Sam's duplicate of mine, which was in his wallet in my purse. I produced it, and without further protest the ticket seller, satisfied with three cards, charged the amount on each one. Such bureaucracy, such stupidity, such a break for us!

Finally we joined the teeming throng and waited for our flight to be posted. People were jammed together like sardines, one section of the terminal crowded with those who looked as though they had come to stay permanently. Whole families were sleeping on the floor, some on rigged up cots and mattresses. Bags of food were shared.

We stood around one of several shoulder-high tables to fill out the custom sheets. We had nothing to declare, but the forms were long and complicated. At last our flight appeared on the board, and we made haste to get in line for the customs officials. Our line stalled. A man ahead of us had failed to make out his papers and was now painstakingly writing. One of his bags would not go through the X-ray trolley. It was a large flat portfolio designed to carry paintings. The guard inspected this bag by hand, then began searching the rest of his baggage with suspicion. Suddenly Aram hissed, "They've caught him. Come with me quickly."

The line next to us had just ended, and we hustled over to it. Aram had seen medals and jewelry pulled from the man's bag. He knew it was contraband and that the man would be stuck with the customs officers for a long time. As we crossed the barrier separating us from the U.S.S.R., I pushed my last thirty rubles into Aram's protesting hand. Without him we well might not have made our exit from Russia. As we made it through customs, Ann cried with relief, "We're out of here! We're free!"

But it wasn't over yet. When we presented our tickets to British Airways, we learned that the flight to Paris was so close on the heels of our arrival in London that we would not have time to reclaim our luggage and buy our fares. The agent offered to call for permission to have our bags checked straight through to Paris so we would not have to spend the night at the airport. She had seen our distress and took pity. Permission was granted. All three of us burst into tears. Here was someone in authority who was willing to bend the rules for us. But she was British.

The relief at leaving Russia was overwhelming. When dinner was served on the plane, we were ecstatic. We raved about the food, realizing we had nearly starved for three weeks. Hearing our expressions of delight, a man sitting in front of us turned around with a laugh and struck up a conversation. He agreed about the Russian food and sympathized when we told him about our disastrous predicament. He even gave us his card and invited us to his home in Scotland if we found ourselves stranded in London.

On landing, we learned the flight to Paris was delayed because of fog. We bought our fares and then sat in the practically empty terminal for two more hours before the boarding sign came up.

We were expecting a Europ Assistance representative to meet us at the airport in Paris to drive us to our hotel, but after claiming our bags, the last ones to appear, we could find no one. It was after midnight. We walked outside to check the cars. There were only a few stragglers and a couple of taxis. I enquired at the British Airways desk whether anyone had asked for us. "Oh, yes," one of them replied, "we paged you at least five times." We had heard nothing.

Fortunately, one taxi was left and the driver was glad to take us to the International Hotel in Neuilly-sur-Seine, where Jeff Kirkman had made our reservations. I told the driver I had no francs, but would pay him when I reached the hotel. He was amenable and understood my rusty French.

All was well when we arrived. Our rooms were ready and we gratefully sank into our beds. It was after 2:00 a.m. and the day had been a nightmare. At 5:30 the phone rang. The hospital was notifying me that the air ambulance had arrived at the airport and would be at the hospital at 6:30 Could we be there to meet it?

I roused Judy and Ann and we hurried into our clothes. It was still quite dark when we reached the street. The desk clerk had given us vague directions and we started out. Somehow a hospital emergency entrance appeared two blocks away, and we rang the night bell. The attendant who answered had no idea why we were there. When we asked if this was the American Hospital, he shook his head. This was not it, and he was unable to tell us where it was so we stumbled on. In the quiet of the night I heard a siren, and we hurried toward the sound. Red lights were flashing up the street, and we ran to catch up. The ambulance turned a corner. We followed it to the emergency entrance of the American Hospital. By the time we reached the ambulance the stretcher was out in front of the doorway.

Sam was completely covered with a stack of blankets, but I knew it was he because his slippers emerged at the end of the cocoon. I was amazed to see him totally swathed in aluminum foil under all the blankets. What an ingenious method of keeping a patient protected from chill and drafts! Sam had not a stitch of clothing. He was unconscious, sedated for the long eight hour flight with two attending doctors and the pilot.

Sam was taken directly to the coronary care unit. We were sent to a waiting room, where we languished for nearly two hours before we were allowed to see him. Sam was conscious, but he appeared very weak and exhausted. We stayed long enough for him to realize we were with him, then left quietly to speak to the doctor.

He was tall, handsome and kind, and spoke English well enough to tell us frankly that Sam's condition was grave. Complications of pneumonia, poor kidney function and circulation were critical. He planned to try another antibiotic to attack the pneumonia virus and do a blood transfusion and tracheotomy as soon as possible so the tube down Sam's throat could be removed. He explained that a week is as long as a tube can be left in the throat. Already Sam's tongue was swollen and blue. It was heartbreaking to see, but he did not seem distressed nor in pain. However, I could not mistake his exhaustion and progressive weakness.

The hospital looked like a chateau to us compared to the run-down antiquated facility in Moscow. Sam lay in a comfortable bed surrounded by up-to-date equipment. His private, curtained room was large and immaculate, with a comfortable chair for a visitor. The nurses stationed outside the door were smiling, helpful and efficient. There was always someone who could speak English, and I could manage a little French. Language was not an impassable barrier as it had been in Russia.

We walked back to the hotel, had breakfast and reviewed our situation yet again. I knew the girls needed to go home and urged them to do so. I could handle the problems here with the help of Europ Assistance. Ann needed to return to her budding business in Boulder. Judy said she would go directly to Indianapolis and take care of some of my business since there was so much to do. Jeff had kept the wires hot across the Atlantic. So many calls came in every day that I only left the room for meals or to visit Sam in the hospital. Jeff made reservations on Air France for Judy and Ann for Saturday.

Everything was easier to cope with in Paris. The International Hotel was close enough to the American Hospital to eliminate the need for taxis. It was small and very comfortable. It was busy and full of clients, but at the same time dignified and quiet. For us it was a haven of comfort and security.

Visiting hours at the hospital were strict. We could see Sam only twice a day for a short time. We found it pleasant to walk the three blocks along the Boulevard Victor Hugo, an important avenue stretching from the Arc de Triomphe into the suburb of Neuilly-sur-Seine. Lovely old trees—horse chestnuts, oaks, beech, maple and elm—formed a veritable umbrella of shade overhead. The trees grew in double rows on either side of the broad sidewalks. Private homes and apartments were secluded by walls with wrought iron gates. This was a street where children played, overseen by their nannies; dogs were exercised by their owners and lovers strolled with arms entwined. Even the traffic moved decorously. Expensive cars with liveried chauffeurs drove in and out of the iron gates enclosing the properties.

The weather was perfect for the end of September, sunny with a crisp bite in the air, a welcome change from the penetrating cold and damp of Moscow. The short walk was refreshing and drove ominous thoughts into dark corners for a while.

On Saturday, a van from Europ Assistance drove the girls to the airport. I went along to see them off. Then the driver took me to the Europ Assistance office to sign some necessary forms.

When I returned to the hotel, desolation settled down on me with a vengeance, but as I took my lonely walk to the hospital, my spirits rose with the invigorating air and the scent of fall. I kicked at the fallen chestnuts and acorns as I strolled. Leaves were beginning to fall, and I picked up a fresh maple leaf, still green and tinged with yellow. Its graceful shape had not yet been distorted by dryness. Boys sped past on roller skates, skirting a frightened poodle leashed to a fashionably dressed lady. An elderly couple, linked arm in arm, took their constitutional. How I envied them!

At the hospital, the nurses tried to rouse Sam, but each day this was increasingly difficult. It was evident he wished to sleep his life away. I could not stay long. It wrenched my heart to see him so spent and wasted. I left after touching his toes at the foot of the bed. At its head, he was surrounded by the intravenous contraption, a respirator and a monitor connected to his heart. It was hard to keep emotion from spilling over. I knew if I broke down I would lose control. I walked back to the hotel and my room, where I could let go in private.

The phone rang, the first of many calls. It was Greg Taggart. He and his French wife live in Paris. They had heard of our disaster from his mother, Towney, a friend in Indianapolis. Greg voiced his sympathy and asked if he and Genevieve could visit me. I was eager for company and insisted they come for dinner.

I hadn't seen Greg since he was a baby in Mexico. Sam had rushed him to the hospital when Towney called in despair to tell us her baby was dying and her doctor gave her no hope. Greg had measles complicated by encephalitis. Our pediatrician pulled him through. Now, forty years later, Greg arrived with his lovely French wife. Genevieve spoke English with difficulty, but was charming and obviously sympathetic to my situation. She was appealing and natural—wore no make-up, not even lipstick. Her hair was straight and long like cornsilk. Greg, quite the opposite, was dark with black expressive eyes. He counterbalanced Genevieve's quiet personality with his vivacious, rather nervous but outgoing manner.

They brought me a Care package, including medicine for my cold, which still had me coughing at night. There were also breakfast biscuits and fruit, as well as a most welcome hair dryer. I was grateful for their gifts and invited them for dinner twice more that week. Alone, I ate practically nothing—just whatever soup was in the daily pot and a fruit compote at lunch and dinner. With Judy and Ann gone, I had continental breakfast in my room.

On Sunday, Sam responded only slightly when the nurse tried to rouse him. His eyes opened. The blue in them had paled to gray. Did he see me? I couldn't tell, but I did know he wasn't fighting any more. He just wanted to sleep. I stroked his forehead and felt the dry flakiness of his skin. The nurse sponged the corners of his mouth where there were raw places from dehydration. His tongue was swollen and discolored. The tracheotomy had not been performed. I caressed his feet at the foot of the bed, then left to consult with the doctor.

He explained that a tracheotomy had not been possible because Sam's blood would not clot. All that night I was tormented by the decision I knew I must make. On Monday morning, I finally met the doctor in charge of Sam's case, the representative from Europ Assistance. He had just returned after a week's vacation. The kind doctor I had been seeing had taken over in his absence.

The new doctor was sympathetic, but was certain Sam could not recover. He did not mince words:

"His kidneys and circulation do not function properly. Heart damage and pneumonia are impossible complications. The only things keeping your husband alive are the drugs and the respirator. Removing either will cause his death."

Although I had almost made my decision, I needed the support of the doctor's words to say it aloud:

"Sam would not want to live this way. I can see him weakening each day. If you can't remove the repirator, do what you can to ease Sam and let him go."

The doctor agreed that was the best decision. He said within forty-eight hours it would all be over.

I left the hospital overcome with grief and despair. I knew I was doing the right thing, but it was terrible to tear him away from life so deliberately. As I walked back to my room, the skies began to weep too, but the umbrella of trees protected me until I was safely inside. The rain then began to fall in earnest. My tears were as heavy.

A family counselor at the hospital was extremely kind and helpful. She spent time with me, giving advice and comfort. I was grateful for her attention. She was an American married to a Frenchman and was worth her weight in gold to me. She stayed by my side when I needed someone to talk to and she helped me when it was all over.

On Wednesday, I sat with Sam for a long time. He was sleeping quietly. As I left, rain began to fall again. The air was tinged with a wintry bite. Sam's raincoat and a scarf, as well as the leafy trees overhead, protected me. Many late September leaves had fallen, turning brown on the pavement. It was hard to keep my thoughts from the impending, inevitable doom. I felt I was fortunate to have had two weeks to prepare for this time.

Fortified with some hot soup, I retired to my room to meditate and pray for strength.

The phone rang at 5:30 Thursday morning. It was September 29, just two weeks to the day since Sam's heart had failed in Moscow. He was gone. I hurried to the hospital, but found Sam's room empty. It was as though no one had ever been in it. The kind, compassionate doctor walked towards me with arms outstretched and tears in his eyes. He enfolded me in a heartfelt embrace, and I broke down, overcome with grief and gratitude for his caring. The nurses gave me Sam's slippers and his few things. I did what I could to thank them for the care they had given him.

After I returned to the hotel, I made and received many phone calls. Jeff Kirkman said Europ Assistance would take me to a location to sign necessary papers. Promptly at 10:00 a.m., the van was at the entrance to the hotel. A nice-looking young man drove me to the city and stopped at a mortuary. I braced myself for the ordeal. I knew what awaited me. I was there for two hours. The mortician was pleasant and, except for filling out the forms, it wasn't as bad as I expected. I felt certain Sam would be well taken care of. They assured me Sam would be home by October 6 at the latest.

I was numb, unable to think clearly, but knew there were things I had to do. Jeff, though across the Atlantic, was by my side taking care of everything. He arranged air reservations and transportation for the next day. I had time to phone Greg and Genevieve to invite them again for dinner and return their hair dryer and other things they had loaned me. I needed companionship. They understood and wanted to be with me also.

On Friday morning, September 30, I was packed and checked out of the hotel by the time the van from Europ Assistance arrived. The young driver escorted me to Orly Airport, took care of my luggage and saw me through the horde of travelers.

Waiting to board seemed endless, but just when I had almost given up hope (I was the last to be called), I was startled to find myself placed in first class. My tickets had been changed from business class because the plane was overbooked. I sat in the most forward seat next to a friendly gentleman from Chicago. It was the most comfortable, luxurious ride on a plane I have ever experienced. Gourmet meals, non-stop champagne, gifts, an orchid corsage and agreeable companionship transformed what would otherwise have been a lonely, self-pitying trip. I arrived home ready and able to face the next sequences with the support of my family.

Remembering my anniversary gift, the ruby earrings, I went to the jewelers to pick them up a few days after my return. Sam's design and the jeweler's workmanship complemented each other perfectly. The earrings are a cherished treasure.

❦

It was hard to embark on a solitary life, especially having to break up our home and move to a retirement center, which I was determined to do. I had decided at least a year before Sam's death that this would be the best plan for my future.

I delayed the inevitable task of disposing of Sam's clothes, but it had to be done. On the top shelf of his closet, I found a small box, wrapped and tied with a red bow. I knew at once it was a Christmas gift for me. I kept the box until Christmas Day. Then, at last, I was ready to open it, although I hated to shatter the beautiful suspense. I thought of Sam's love for me and his preparing for my Christmas so far ahead. It was a tender, prayerful moment as I loosened the fancy red bow and peeled back the silver paper.

I was sitting with Ann in her bedroom in Boulder early Christmas morning. I wanted her to share this moment with me. Choking back tears, I pulled off the lid. Then I cried until I thought I would never stop. What I saw was a tiny ruby pendant that matched the earrings. Once around my neck it has stayed there—a talisman of Sam and his love.

How lucky I felt to receive such a tangible gift. It was as though Sam were still with me—still thinking of me. His presence was real then and still is, communicating to me in my thoughts.

Sam Moxley in the nineteen-seventies.

Sam and Lucina at the National Association of Chain Drug Stores convention in Hawaii, 1985.

On board the *U.S.S. Independence* en route to Las Palmas, Mallorca, Spain 1967.

On board the *Rhapsody* in the Caribbean for a music festival cruise, 1986.

At home for Christmas, 1987.

Sam and Lucina greeting Clifford Tretich, flutist. Clifford, an Aspen Scholarship winner, was the guest artist for an organization's benefit recital at Fairview Presbyterian Church.

Pia Sebastiani, the pianist for our "soiree," Februrary 14, 1988.

Ruth Slenczynska, the pianist for another "soiree," January 17, 1988.

On board the *Royal Viking Sea* from Rio de Janiero, Brazil, December, 1988. Farthest from the camera are the James Pattersons. Sam is in a wheel chair, having lost some circulation in his leg, and we are waiting to disembark from Belem for Indianapolis.

Our two guides in the U.S.S.R. Both of them named Marina. September, 1988.

A view from the palace, Petrodvorets, showing the distance from the Neva River and the walkway along the canal.

Sam and Lucina in Leningrad, September, 1988. Behind us is Dr. Frankel, one of the doctors who gave CPR to Sam in the bus.

Sam and Judy with one of our directors, Phillip Ryan. Leningrad, U.S.S.R.

Lucina, Judy and Ann having tea in the log house near Sochi.

Ann at balustrade overlooking Yerevan, Armenia.

Lucina and Judy in Leningrad before boarding the hydrofoil to Petrodvorets.

The Russian sign translates "Emergency Entrance." It is the hospital in Moscow, September 15, 1988.

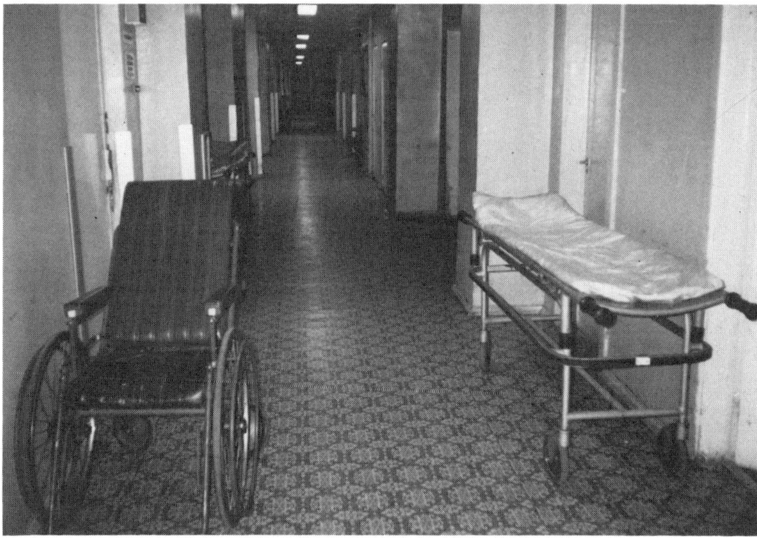

Interior of the hospital showing a corridor and section of bathroom.

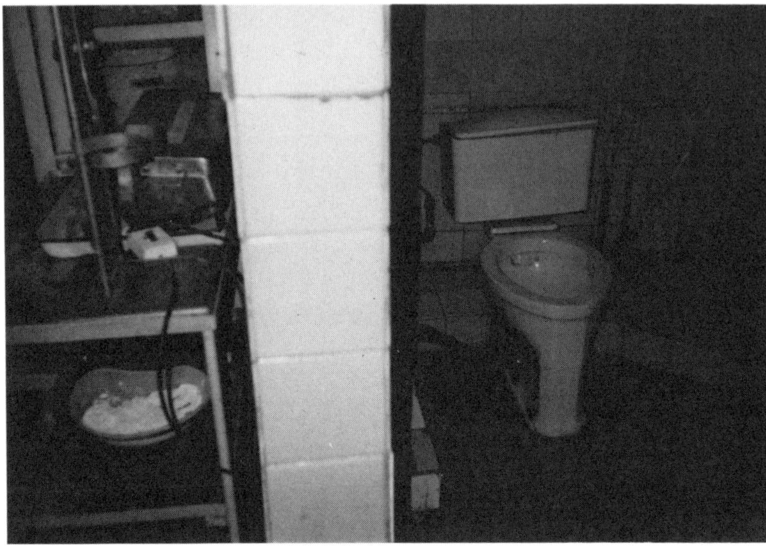

More views of the antiquated bathroom in very poor condition.

Our twenty-fifth anniversary was spent at our cottage in Culver, where we were married in 1948. Sophie, our treasured poodle, is on my lap.